Queering the English Language Classroom

Queering the English Language Classroom

A Practical Guide for Teachers

Joshua M. Paiz

SHEFFIELD UK BRISTOL CT

Published by Equinox Publishing Ltd.
UK: Office 415, The Workstation, 15 Paternoster Row, Sheffield, South Yorkshire S1 2BX
USA: ISD, 70 Enterprise Drive, Bristol, CT 06010

www.equinoxpub.com

First published 2020

ISBN-13 978 1 78179 793 8 (hardback)
978 1 78179 794 5 (paperback)
978 1 78179 795 2 (ePDF)

British Library Cataloguing-in-Publication Data

A catalogue record for this book is available from the British Library.

Library of Congress Cataloging-in-Publication Data

Names: Paiz, Joshua M., author.
Title: Queering the English language classroom : a practical guide for teachers / Joshua M. Paiz.
Description: Sheffield, South Yorkshire ; Bristol, CT : Equinox Publishing Ltd, 2020. | Includes bibliographical references and index. | Summary: "This book provides recommendations on how to make the classroom more inclusive by discussing strategies for selecting inclusive curricular content, and also contains advice to teachers on how to handle student and institutional resistance to creating queer inclusive spaces"—Provided by publisher.
Identifiers: LCCN 2020010125 (print) | LCCN 2020010126 (ebook) | ISBN 9781781797938 (hardback) | ISBN 9781781797945 (paperback) | ISBN 9781781797952 (ebook)
Subjects: LCSH: English language—Study and teaching—Foreign speakers. | Sexual orientation—Study and teaching. | Homosexuality and education. | Queer theory.
Classification: LCC PE1128.A2 P275 2020 (print) | LCC PE1128.A2 (ebook) |
DDC 428.0071—dc23
LC record available at https://lccn.loc.gov/2020010125
LC ebook record available at https://lccn.loc.gov/2020010126

Typeset by JS Typesetting Ltd, Porthcawl, Mid Glamorgan

For Bin, your love and patience made this possible.
For Emily, your encouragement kept me going.

Contents

Preface

As a writer and a reader, I feel like prefaces are strange things—oft-ignored, but actually quite useful. I have, however, included *this* preface because I feel it may help you to decide if you want to buy/rent this book and whether you will find it at all useful. So, here's what you'll get out of reading this preface: a general introduction to the topic of this book; a statement of why this topic matters and warrants your careful consideration as a practitioner (the exigency); an understanding of how I am positioned relative to this book and how that positioning impacts this work (the positionality statement); and an overview of this book to help guide your reading of it.

A Brief Introduction to LGBTQ+ Issues in English Language Teaching

LGBTQ+ issues have slowly risen to disciplinary awareness, greatly aided by what David Block (2003) refers to as the social turn in second language acquisition. A key moment in the field's cognisance of LGBTQ+ issues was during the 1992 TESOL convention in Vancouver, British Columbia. During this meeting, Cynthia Nelson (1993) and some of her colleagues organized a colloquium called, 'We are Your Colleagues: Lesbians and Gays in ESL' (Carscadden, Ward, and Nelson 1992). In this colloquium, Nelson and her co-organizers would call out the rampant heterosexism in the field of English language teaching (ELT), going so far as to say that all practitioners, researchers, scholars, administrators, and most importantly students, were treated as straight until—and sometimes even if—proven otherwise (Nelson 1993). In a subsequent *TESOL Quarterly* forum article, she outlined seven attitudes that were endemic to ELT and TESOL at the time that created an atmosphere of invisibility for LGBTQ+-identified individuals.

Following this watershed moment, LGBTQ+ issues would fall dormant until the late 1990s and the publication of a group of articles on identity in *TESOL Quarterly*. In 1997, Stephanie Vandrick published 'The Role of Hidden Identities in the Postsecondary ESL Classroom.' In this article, she discussed how sexual identities, along with others, such as immigrant and socioeconomic identities, may be hidden in educational contexts because of threats to the students' sense of self, perceived or actual. Groundbreaking in this work was Vandrick's attention to the effects of the intersectionality of different identities. That is, we cannot just excise out sexual identity as a focus for inquiry or pedagogical intervention. Rather, we must consider how identities interact with one another and how they become salient in communicative and educational encounters. While this book will focus on sexual identity, it will attempt to give that same consideration to the intersectionality of sexual identities with racial, socioeconomic, political, religious, and gender identities.

More recently, there has been a considerable expansion of LGBTQ+-focused work appearing in journals like *TESOL Quarterly, TESOL Journal,* the *Journal of Language, Identity, and Education,* and the *Journal of Language and Sexuality*. Additionally, professional organizations and meetings such as the ILGBTQF professional leaning network of the TESOL International Association and the Lavender Language and Linguistics conference have created additional disciplinary space for work focused on LGBTQ+ issues in ELT. This work has focused on everything from introducing LGBTQ+ material to classrooms in so-called frigid institutional climates (e.g. faith-based colleges in Japan; Ó'Móchain 2006) to building specialized programmes for LGBTQ+ language learners (Merse 2015; Moore 2016) and tackling heteronormative curricular materials that present a white-washed, monosexual world that renders sexual minorities as invisible, if not fictional (Motschenbacher 2010; Paiz 2015a). I will present a more detailed overview of this work in chapter one, but for now, this brief history serves to contextualize the disciplinary moment in which this book is situated.

Exigency Statement

Given growing interest in diversity, equity, and inclusion in ELT and related fields, it is important to acknowledge the exigencies that have driven me to write this book. I am writing this book because I strongly believe that it is needed. First and foremost, identity matters in language learning and acquisition. It can drive people to want to learn new languages, and it can motivate people to acquire greater proficiencies in a language (see Block

2007; Paiz 2015b). Enough interest has been generated by identity-based research that scores of scholarly books and identity-focused journals have launched over the past twenty years. This state of affairs speaks, I feel, to the role that identity considerations can play in the language classroom.

More specifically, lesbian, gay, bisexual, transgender, queer, et alia (LGBTQ+) identities have received increased scholarly attention in recent years, in part because of the increased visibility of LGBTQ+ peoples in the public sphere. However, how does this fact make sexual identity relevant to the realm of language education? I think that the statistics regarding LGBTQ+ youth and young adults and bullying, suicide, homelessness, and substance abuse speak to the need to prepare teachers to work with, and to create space for, language learners that not only identify with the LGBTQ+ community, but that will be interacting with LGBTQ+ people in their daily lives. Failure to adequately prepare educators to queer their practice reinforces the invisibility of LGBTQ+ populations (see also Paiz 2018); and, when this occurs students feel shut out of the educational space because they do not see viable or preferred identity positions being made available to them. Moreover, there are real consequences for LGBTQ+ youth and young adult learners. For example, by allowing heteronormative, if not downright homophobic, views to go unchallenged in our institutions and classrooms we leave the door open to damaging and dangerous behaviours such as bullying, substance abuse, and more. These environmental and behavioural factors can then feed into youth suicide and homelessness—bear in mind that suicide is the second leading cause of death among LGBTQ+ youth (Centers for Disease Control and Prevention 2017), and almost 40% of homeless youth in the United States are LGBTQ+-identified (Durso and Gates 2012). So, being able to create queered language education spaces is an important and worthwhile task. It is important for LGBTQ+ language learners who might want to integrate into language-specific LGBTQ+ communities, and it is important for non-LGBTQ+ language learners to be better able to interact respectfully with LGBTQ+ individuals.

Positionality Statement

Any work is necessarily 'stained' by its author. That is, everything is biased, and so is this book. The work presented in it is certainly liberal in its orientation, and some may say that parts are radically so. It must be, as it is aligned with a social justice view of the fields of ELT, teaching English to speakers of other languages (TESOL), and applied linguistics (ALx) through its connections to various left-leaning theories (i.e. queer theory). So, I acknowledge now that there will be bias in this book. I will, however, attempt to control for that bias in two ways. First, I will, where appropriate, give some voice to other perspectives—even if I disagree with them wholly. Second, I will be honest about who I am as an author—as a person and as a professional. The second part, I will take care of in this section—so that you are not reading a constant autobiography, which is not why you are here.

So, my name is Joshua M. Paiz. I am a married, cis-gender, gay man that grew up in the American Midwest in a biracial (my mum is Caucasian American, and my dad is a third or fourth generation Mexican American), conservative, evangelical Christian home. And, I tend to lean further and further left on most social issues as I get older, recently being called a radical leftist by one of my colleagues. I hold a doctorate in second language studies/TESOL from Purdue University where many of my professors could be described as also being leftists engaged in work in the areas of critical applied linguistics and World Englishes. I have been doing work related to LGBTQ+ issues in the field for about five years (as of 2020) with published work on the topic appearing in *TESOL Journal*, the *Journal of Language and Sexuality*, the *Journal of Language, Identity and Education*, and various smaller regional outlets. I have strong opinions about this topic, which is why I am writing this book. That being said, my conservative past means that I am at times conflicted when it comes to the most ethical and culturally responsive way to do so.

I have been in and out of the closet numerous times before finally settling on being out and marrying my husband. For me, carry out scholarly inquiry in the area of LGBTQ+ issues in ELT has allowed me to not only find a place in my field and a voice with which to speak, it has also enabled me to make peace with my own sexual identity and to understand better its role in my teaching and my efforts as a second language learner (of Mandarin Chinese). This topic is very near to me. However, I do not own this topic. No matter how heavily invested in it I may be. So in the act of writing this book, I bring with me not only my liberal, leftist professional self; I also bring with me that conservative past, inherited as it was from my parents who have variously been police officers, deputy sheriffs, janitors, and factory workers. So, there may be moments of tension and even contradiction in the following pages; and, that, to me, is perfectly natural.

Book Overview

This book is broken into seven chapters that will provide you with an overview of LGBTQ+ work in the fields of TESOL and ALx and will provide a working toolkit for queering the English language classroom. Being an educator myself, I have attempted to make this book as accessible to the practitioner as possible. That means that I have attempted to maintain a more accessible tone and approach to help the busy practitioner read, reflect, and possibly integrate the recommendations of this book into their practice. To help you consider how the ideas advanced in this book might interface with your own practice, each chapter will conclude with a 'reflexive praxis prompt'. These prompts have been designed to help you take the time to think about your own experiences and beliefs in dialogue with the pedagogical approach advocated for herein. Now, if you are exceptionally busy and do not have time or energy to read this whole book, here are the highlights of each chapter.

Chapter 1 introduces queer theory as it relates to the fields of TESOL and ALx. It then establishes the need to queer the English language classroom in a way that creates an educational space that is inclusive of LGBTQ+ and other marginalized students. This chapter concludes by operationalising the term 'queer' as a verb. This definitional work is geared towards providing practitioners with a tool-for-thought that they can use to queer their practice. Doing so will allow them to create classroom spaces that engage with dominant social discourses in such a way that the discursive construction of *all* identities is made salient for students. Moreover, this work allows educators to help students problematize and resist marginalising discourses by making space for non-heteronormative sexual identities.

Chapter 2 applies recent advances in LGBTQ+ studies in TESOL/ALx to update and extend Cynthia Nelson's notion of queer inquiry (2006, 2009) as introduced in Chapter 1. It then provides practical recommendations for how to construct a queer inquiry-based pedagogy that fits one's contextual needs (e.g. national and institutional). This chapter includes both guiding questions for those who have just begun to consider queering their practice, and critical reflective questions for those who have already started queering their classroom spaces.

Chapter 3 highlights how using queer inquiry-based pedagogies troubles normative spaces and the identity options that they create for students. It begins by revisiting some of the significant issues created by heteronormative classrooms. It then outlines ways that the educator can model the troubling of and resistance to those normative discourses. It focuses on developing LGBTQ+-inclusive lesson plans and assignments, favouring the localized approach advanced by Robert Ó'Móchain (2006). This approach advocates for embedding efforts to queer the language classroom in the local context, as this provides students with a more accessible route to engage with LGBTQ+ topics.

Chapter 4 begins by discussing how many mainstream curricular materials (e.g. textbooks, media, etc.) present students with heteronormative views of the world. It then highlights how this heteronormativity can create issues in the language learning classroom. The discussion then moves on to present how to purposefully queer existing curricular materials so that students can begin to explore both linguistic and cultural issues related to LGBTQ+ identity options in their local context. This chapter also returns to the work of Robert Ó'Móchain (2006), Greg Curran (2006), and Thorsten Merse (2014, 2015) to provide a practical framework for developing one's own, locally relevant materials to help make classrooms more LGBTQ+ inclusive in non-normative ways.

Chapter 5 expands on current queer and LGBTQ+ work in fields related to ELT by addressing the need to integrate queer perspectives into the classroom in a critical fashion. It also provides a holistic guide to assessing students' varied reactions to the queered educational space, with an eye towards using guided reflections to help teachers plan future sessions that deal with LGBTQ+ content/themes. Additionally, Chapter 5 will present recommendations for how to address institutional, parental, and student resistance in queering the language classroom.

Chapter 6 discusses possible goals and outcomes for the queered language learning space. It also provides reflective prompts to think of how to (a) fit queer practices into current courses' goals and outcomes and (b) how to develop locally relevant goals and outcomes that address students' lived experiences.

Chapter 7 ties together the discussion that has taken place in the previous six chapters and provides a rough outline for future work in both the classroom and in the discipline through continued research, scholarship, and materials creation/curriculum design. The book closes out with a short Afterword that acknowledges the challenges of addressing LGBTQ+ issues in so-called frigid climates. That is, how do we meaningfully address queer issues in religious schools, or national contexts that view queer lives as aberrant? This final note is being included because much of the queer work in TESOL, ELT, and ALx fails to take this matter into account fully.

List of Abbreviations

AAAL	American Association for Applied Linguistics
ALx	applied linguistics
CCCC	Conference on College Composition and Communication
EAL	English as an additional language
EAP	English for academic purposes
EFL	English as a foreign language
ELL	English as an additional language
ELT	English language teaching
ESL	English as a second language
ESP	English for specific purposes
GCE	Global Citizenship Education
HRC	The Human Rights Campaign
IEP	intensive English programme
L2	second language
LGBTQ+	lesbian, gay, bisexual, transgender, queer, questioning, two-spirited, same-sex loving, intersexed, asexual, etc.
NYU	New York University
OER	Open Educational Resource
SLA	second language acquisition
TESOL	Teaching English to Speakers of other languages (also TESOL International Association)

1

What is 'Queering' and Why Should We All Do It?

AT A GLANCE

Introduction

This chapter will give you the background you need to better position your (queered) practice in the context of broader disciplinary discussions on LGBTQ+ issues in English language teaching (ELT). This chapter will include a working definition of what LGBTQ+/Queer TESOL scholars mean when we talk about 'queering' ELT practice. The goal here is to provide you with tools-for-thought that you can use as you critically reflect on your practice and how it addresses issues of identity as they come up in the classroom—and note that this does not just mean issues of sexual identity. After reading this chapter, you should be able to better integrate a queer-informed approach into your teaching philosophy. In Chapter 2, the focus will shift to a description of queer inquiry-based pedagogies. Before

I go any further, however, I must provide you with a proviso due to the complex, often fraught nature of sexuality in education.

> **Proviso:** There is more than one way to queer ELT practice. What I will present here will be a set of best practices based on my time carrying out research and scholarship in the area of queer TESOL/lavender applied linguistics, as well as my own—sometimes tentative and unsuccessful—attempts to queer my own practice as a university practitioner that has worked in both North American and Chinese contexts.

There is a straightforward reason why I believe that we should all work to queer our classroom practice, which I will explore throughout this chapter. For now, a good summary of my position would be this: I believe that identity issues—whether it is grounded in class, race, gender, sexuality, religion, politics, and so on—can have profound impacts on second language learning and acquisition. It can be the reason why students begin learning an additional language—as in the case of Han, a transgender student discussed by Nguyen and Yang (2015)—or it can, when even incidentally resisted by the teacher, serve to silence students or to cast them as deficient language learners (see Liddicoat 2009). Because of this fact, it is imperative that we consider how matters of identity in classroom contexts, including sexual identity, affect our attempts to create validating and accepting educational spaces that facilitate language learning. Given the amount of time many English language (EL) teachers spend with their students, there is the possibility that regressive, marginalizing classroom discourses may have a disproportionate effect for English as an additional language (EAL) students, especially for LGBTQ+ EAL students.

Before providing an extended discussion on LGBTQ+ considerations in the fields of TESOL and applied linguistics (ALx), let us begin with a working definition of the term 'queering' and what it means in the ELT context. Elsewhere, I have defined *queering the English language classroom* as the use of pedagogical strategies and curricular materials that trouble all identities, not just sexual ones, and how they are performed through language during communicative events. Moreover, queering educational practice attempts to create lessons that make clear to students the ways that they are positioned by dominant social discourses and expectations that, in effect, 'police' the identity options available to them (see also Paiz 2018). Queering our practice is done to help students to talk about the inequalities and marginalization that they or those close to them may face by being minority, female, lower-language proficiency, or LGBTQ+. Queering the classroom is built on critical inquiry and inclusive curricular materials (see Nelson 2006; Paiz 2015a, 2018). Throughout this book, we will return to the concept of queering and explore practical ways to build inclusive classroom spaces. Here, however, it may be helpful to differentiate some of the ways that forms of the word 'queer' will be used in this book, in keeping with accepted approaches from critical ALx and queer theory. Throughout this book, the verb 'to queer' can perhaps best be understood as a sort of restive problematizing (see also Pennycook 2001), one that focuses on questioning how society and language predispose us to favour monogamous, procreative, heterosexual pairings as normal and desirable. Meanwhile, the adjectival form, 'queered' can best be understood as a (site of) practice that has already been troubled in some way so as to make that space more accessible to and equitable for sexual minorities.

This chapter will begin by discussing the seminal moments in TESOL and ALx that helped to bring LGBTQ+ issues to the attention of these two fields. The starting point in this review will be the 1992 colloquium on LGBTQ+ practitioners and researchers that was held during that year's TESOL Convention (Carscadden, Ward, and Nelson 1992; Nelson 1993), which served as historical starting point for this topic and called out heteronormative bias in the field. Then, I will discuss some of the studies on LGBTQ+ issues that came out in the early 2000s, during a period of increasing focus on LGBTQ+ issues in the language classroom, focused mostly on the student, their willingness to engage with LGBTQ+ content, and the challenges that educators faced in doing so. This review will include insights from Greg Curran (2006) about the challenges that out members of the LGBTQ+ community face when attempting to address queer issues in the language classroom. It will also include a look at how young learners engage with LGBTQ+ themes both in and out of the classroom, as reported by Luiz Paolo Moita-Lopes (2006), who was examining EFL classrooms in the Brazilian context. Then, this chapter will explore recent developments in Queer TESOL/Lavender ALx that have looked at topics ranging from curriculum design (Merse 2015; Moore 2016), normative curricular materials (Motschenbacher 2010; Paiz 2015a), as well as the areas that the field has mostly left unexplored, such as bisexual and transgender issues (Nguyen and Yang 2015). The chapter will close by roughly outlining what queer-informed pedagogies look like, before inviting you to critically reflect on this chapter in dialogue with your practice as an ELT educator.

The Early Days of Queer TESOL

To understand more fully what is meant by queering ELT and what is at stake in normative classes, we must first understand how this topic rose to an area of interest in the field. Recently, Queer TESOL/Lavender ALx have both been identified as growing subfields with a diverse and expanding body of literature (Leap and Motschenbacher 2012; Leap 2013). For our purposes, we can identify the emergence of a disciplinary interest in LGBTQ+ issues to the early 1990s when *TESOL Quarterly* published a forum piece based on an earlier TESOL convention panel (Carscadden, Ward, and Nelson 1992; Nelson 1993). In this forum piece, entitled 'Heterosexism in ESL: Examining our Attitudes', Cynthia Nelson (1993: 143) began with a proverbial shot across the discipline's bow, stating clearly and directly, 'We are your colleagues ... lesbians and gays in TESOL'. This bold opening called immediate attention to an invisibility and silencing of LGBTQ+ identified professionals (and students) that had been endemic in the field up to that point. Nelson tied this invisibility to seven attitudes that she saw as perpetuating an environment of heterosexism in the field. *Heterosexism*, which would later come to be known in part as heteronormativity, referred to the view that the field of TESOL, its practitioners, its scholars, its researchers, its administrators, and—most importantly—its students were straight until, and sometimes even if, proven otherwise. Because of how groundbreaking this piece was, and how important it remains, I want to review some Nelson's (1993) seven heterosexist attitudes—in part because you will likely still encounter them when talking with your colleagues and school/programme administrators, as I have during academic debates and training sessions (i.e. Pandavar and Paiz 2017; Francis, Hseih, and Paiz 2017).

- Attitude 1: We are all teachers so why does sexual identity matter at all? (Nelson 1993: 144). On the surface, there is nothing wrong with this attitude. We are professionals, and it is our professional identity that should be the most salient and important in the classroom, correct? Simply put, no. As Nelson quite rightly points out, we cannot walk away from our sexual identities any more than we can from our cultural, gender, or ethnic identities. It is just that straight-identified teachers have the benefit of living with an unmarked sexual identity. That is, their sexual identity matches the tacit societal norm and therefore goes unquestioned.

- Attitude 2: Sexuality and sexual identity should not come up in the classroom through a teacher's purposeful efforts, nor should it be allowed to come up incidentally through student contributions (Nelson 1993: 145–146). This attitude is entirely wrong. Sexuality does come up in the English language classroom, and it does so in a myriad of ways. It can come up during conversations about what someone has planned for the weekend. It can come up as a student discusses a recently married family member. Also, it can come up when one student calls another student's actions 'gay', using it as a stand-in for the word stupid. Sexuality comes up in our classes, even if we are not listening (see Moita-Lopes 2006). So, we must be prepared to engage with it.
- Attitude 3: Talking about LGBTQ+ issues is too controversial for the language classroom (Nelson 1993: 146). We already tackle controversial topics in the language classroom. So, we would be doing our students a disservice if we shied away from issues of sexuality. So, if we can feel comfortable teaching other critical cultural topics (e.g. the one/two child policy in China, gun control in the US), then sexuality and sexual identity must not be any different, especially if we want to practice a critically informed, liberatory pedagogy.
- Attitude 5: I never say anything against LGBTQ+ individuals or anything at all about this topic, so why should it matter (Nelson 1993: 147)? This is an attitude that can be particularly infuriating because it is predicated on the false assumption that neutrality is an option in education. That not taking a stance can somehow shield us from making ideological or political statements. This is not true, and our students do not

see it as true either (see Barnard 1994; Rivers 2001, 2004). All teaching is always already ideologically fraught and politically situated.

- Attitude 7: Only LGBTQ+ people can teach about LGBTQ+ issues (Nelson 1993: 149). The logic that drives this attitude would discount many native English speakers from teaching ESL/EFL classes if they had never learned a second language to a comparable proficiency level as their students before. Likewise, it would mean that only people with happy, successful marriages could teach units on marriage and romance. What this attitude is masking is a teacher's latent discomfort with addressing LGBTQ+ topics in the classroom. Moreover, as we will see in later sections of this chapter, research shows us that LGBTQ+ identified teachers often face additional challenges bringing up LGBTQ+ content in the classroom (see Curran 2006; Vandrick 2001).

Many of the attitudes summarized above advocate for a seemingly acceptable stance of distance and neutrality. Critical educators, however, can see that when we attempt to take a neutral path, our students often see it as a tacit endorsement of the status quo, of heteronormative, marginalizing discourses that may be sidelining either themselves, their friends, or their loved ones (Barnard 1994; Rivers 2001, 2004). Moreover, this can have profound impacts on language learning and teaching by creating environments that encourage some to disengage, to fall silent, because they feel that they do not have the right to speak.

After Cynthia Nelson's rather direct wake-up call for the field, Stephanie Vandrick (1997) directed its attention to how sexual identity and unwelcoming educational spaces might impact students and learning. By discussing what she termed *hidden identities*, Vandrick was able to highlight what is at stake affectively and educationally for students who feel othered or marginalized because of how socially significant others (e.g. parents, friends, teachers, etc.) could position them. When speaking specifically of LGBTQ+ identities, she pointed out that the fear of being outed to parents or becoming the target of bullying could lead students to want to hide their sexual identities. This justifiable concern could become affectively draining for them in the classroom, where they may have to choose between performing their authentic sexual identity or masking it during activities that ask seemingly benign questions like, 'What did you do over the weekend?' or 'Are you seeing anyone?' (see also Curran 2002; Saunston 2016; Watson, Wheldon, and Russell 2015).

For Vandrick (1997), whether or not a student would choose to hide a given identity—whether it be sexual, religious, political, socioeconomic, ethnic, etc.—was primarily grounded in issues of power and ideology that they felt permeated the educational space. More specifically, the worry that some form of censure, silencing, or harm could come from self-disclosure may lead students to elect to hide a facet of their identity. Stepping away from sexual identity, a wealthy student worried about ostracization from their peer group may choose to enact a more middle-class social identity in the classroom. Fearing outing from the authority figure in the classroom (the teacher) the student may go to great lengths to hide their wealthy socioeconomic identity. For example, losing announcements about parent career share days, wearing off-brand or discount store brand clothing, or mirroring the speech markers of students from lower socioeconomic backgrounds (cf. Ortmeier-Hooper 2008). Vandrick (1997) maintains that all of this 'hiding' can have negative impacts on students' educational attainment, in part because of the extra affective and cognitive effort that the student has to expend in maintaining false fronts.

To counter the negative impacts of students' hidden identities, she advocated for teachers actively taking steps to create safe and inclusive classrooms. She, as do I, admitted that there is no silver bullet, no magical set of steps to take to guarantee that every classroom is non-marginalizing and nurturing (Vandrick 1997: 156–157). However, she did acknowledge that this work of creating safe educational spaces requires educators and administrators to seek to counter marginalizing discourses. Doing so may mean that inclusive curricular materials need to be used in the classroom (see Chapter 4), or that negative language and bullying must directly be met by the educator and the institution with restorative and progressive policies that help all parties understand the importance of inclusive and validating dialogue and engagement. That is, it is not about enforcing conformity or tolerance. It is about modelling respectful ways of disagreement and difference.

Once LGBTQ+ issues were brought to disciplinary attention—once we as professionals were forced to consider the impacts of heteronormative behaviours on our fellow professionals and students—we had no choice but to integrate them more fully into the research agenda of ELT. This led to considerable growth in the body of research and scholarly arguments during the 2000s and 2010s, a trend that continues today. In the next section, I look at this early explosion more closely, focusing on the deepening of our understanding of LGBTQ+ identities and student and teacher issues.

Picking Up Steam: Expanding Inquiry

After Nelson (1993, 1999) and Vandrick (1997) broached LGBTQ+ issues as legitimate disciplinary concerns, the first decade of the 21st century would see considerable efforts being made to understand how advances from queer theory and LGBT studies could inform ELT practice and shed light on the scope of the problems created by normative classroom spaces. The goal of the agenda that guided researchers from 2000–2010 seemed to be about understanding how sexuality, ELT, and ALx intersected, paying attention to the effects of normative discourses on classroom practice and curricular materials (e.g. De Vincenti, Giovanangeli, and Ward 2007; Liddicoat 2009; Moita-Lopes 2006), how queer theory could drive inclusive language teaching pedagogy (Nelson 2002, 2006, 2009; Ó'Móchain 2006); what drove students to desire inclusive classroom spaces (Curran 2006; King 2008), as well as what remained to be understood in order to better serve EL students, some of whom may be members of this marginalized population (Cameron 2005). In this section, I will discuss each of these topic areas in turn. The purpose behind this extensive review is to increase awareness around the complexities of queering the English language classroom and of creating appropriately inclusive educational spaces for all students, including marginalized sexual minorities.

Normative Practices

This first example is, to me, one of the starkest examples of the potential damages caused by normative classroom practices. It is helpful, here, to recall that heteronormative practices are those that either directly, or indirectly, silence and make invisible LGBTQ+ lives by presenting heterosexuality as the only natural and acceptable sexual identity. Liddicoat's (2009) 'Sexual Identity as Linguistics Failure' painted a stark picture of what happens when language learners are in heteronormative classrooms. He looked specifically at the Japanese and Spanish as a foreign language classrooms (JFL/SFL). However, his findings are readily generalizable to the English as a second language/foreign language (ESL/EFL) classrooms as well. What he found was that in the classes that he observed students who performed LGBTQ+ identities—ones that did not fit normative expectations—were cast as deficient students, failing to grasp important lessons about grammar, lexis, and socioculturally specific language use. For example, in the SFL classroom, the teacher asked a male student to describe his girlfriend. When the student supplied *mi novio es alto y delgado* (my boyfriend is tall and handsome), the teacher assumed the student failed to grasp how Spanish marks gender through the morphemes [a] for feminine/female and [o] for masculine/male (Liddicoat 2009: 195). The teacher then recasts the student's sentence to be all feminine (i.e. *mi novia es alta y delgada* – my girlfriend is tall and handsome). The student, attempting to resist the heterosexual identification of the teacher, recasts the teachers statement to be *mi novio es alta y delgada*, assuming that the error was in using the masculine ending on the two adjectives. The student's attempted recast led to a legitimate error, which the teacher then corrected, again to the heteronormative response assuming a mixed gender couple.

Here, the student's attempt to perform a minority sexual identity led to the teacher assuming the student failed to grasp core linguistic concepts, positioning the student as a deficient language learner. When the student attempted to resist this, it led to a legitimate error and the continuation of the normative practices of the teacher. Over time, this action can have silencing effects for LGBTQ+ students, disinviting them from fully and authentically participating in the educational space. This lack of engagement can, over the longer term, have profoundly negative impacts on the learner and their attempts to learn an additional language. Faced with such an environment, many LGBTQ+ language learners must choose between challenging the teacher, accepting the identity of a straight student to better fit with heteronormative discourses, deflecting the invitation to participate in course activities, or withdrawing from the educational space all together.

Moita-Lopes (2006) extends the examination into the K-12 context in Brazil and explores student attitudes towards LGBTQ+ issues, as well as what happens when teachers choose not to engage with issues of sexuality, sexual literacy, and troubling normative discourses. Perhaps one of the most important findings of Moita-Lopes's research was that students, even at the middle school level, expressed interest in having classroom materials that included some discussion of LGBTQ+ topics. This desire was motivated by either the students' own sexual identity or because they had friends or family members that identified as LGBTQ+. However, some teachers aggressively resisted including LGBTQ+-focused discussions into the classroom because of concerns that ranged from the political to the pedagogical. However, when teachers took this stance—of either active or passive non-engagement—it pushed the discussions of LGBTQ+ matters outside of the classroom and into the hallways, cafeterias, playgrounds, and locker rooms. In these settings, where there was little-to-no adult supervision, he found that normative, and frequently downright homophobic, discourses took root. For example, in one classroom interaction, students talked about how men with effeminate sounding voices must have some issue that makes them 'not normal' (Moita-Lopes 2006: 39). In the vignette that he focused on, this discussion of some abstract gay man turned towards the group's classmate and led to a conversation that could feed into the bullying of the targeted student because the student in question spoke 'in a totally different way ... walks in a different way ... [because] he wiggles his ass [when he walks]' (ibid.).

Additionally, Moita-Lopes also examined problematic curricular materials at his research sites. What he found was that when textbooks did include LGBTQ+ content, the textbook authors did so in a way that reinforced negative stereotypes about LGBTQ+ individuals. In one such textbook, he found a reprinted news story about an army officer that was caught engaging in a sexual affair with another man (Moita-Lopes 2006: 44). He contended that this presentation was predicated on dominant social discourses of gay men as sexually hyperactive and preying on other men. Chapter 4 will discuss ways of troubling materials like this one. Suffice it to say, however, that when texts like the one that Moita-Lopes (ibid.) encountered are used and not troubled for the students, they continue to feed into marginalizing views of LGBTQ+ individuals that can have profound impacts for language learners.

Normative Materials

The early 2000s saw TESOL and Appling Linguistics researchers paying additional attention to the role of curricular materials in propping up marginalizing heteronormative discourses. De Vincenti, Giovanangeli, and Ward (2007), in their review of French, Italian, and Japanese textbooks, reported on some of the problems with commercially available materials that, if left untroubled, would lead to issues with creating inclusive classroom spaces. They reported many cases of the total absence of LGBTQ+ characters, issues, or authors in the textbooks. What is more troubling, however, is that they also found examples of texts where LGBTQ+ themes or characters were included but were done in exceedingly negative ways. For example, one of the French language textbooks in their sample presented gay men in such a way that it perpetuated the notion that they were all diseased individuals (De Vincenti, Giovanangeli, and Ward 2007: 64). Shardakova and Pavlenko (2004) further underscored the issue with normative, or even homophobic, materials of this nature. They correctly pointed out that the textbooks that we use, and the characters and stories that populate them, begin to present to the learner a range of available identity options—ways of being—that the target culture values (see also Gray 2013; Motschenbacher 2010). So, the erasure or stigmatizing presentation of LGBTQ+ lives in curricular materials can suggest to students that there is no space for LGBTQ+ lives in the target culture. Given that early-service teachers tend to over-rely on textbooks, this problem is made even more profound (see Ball and Feiman-Menser 1988; Grossman and Thompson 2008).

The early 2000s provided profound insight into the problems of normative classrooms and materials. It also showed us the potential pedagogical pitfalls of an uncritical, unpurposeful attempt to queer ELT practice (see Curran 2006). To begin redressing this problem, Cynthia Nelson (2006, 2007, 2009) began taking the early steps to outline how purposefully infusing queer theory into ELT could serve as a guide to meaningfully queering practice. In the next section, I will discuss Cynthia Nelson's queer inquiry approach in greater detail, as it also serves as part of the foundation of the approach advocated for throughout this book.

Queer Theory and ELT

Throughout the early 2000s, Cynthia Nelson began building the case that queer theory had the potential to inform ELT practice in ways that could lead to the use of what Deborah Britzman (1995) had termed 'pedagogies of inclusion'. She argued that the focus on linguistic and cultural diversity in the English language classroom made it the prime place to deploy a queer theory-informed pedagogy that could lay bare the ways that societies value certain identities and identity expressions over others (Nelson 2002: 44). By raising students' awareness of the ways that cultural groups value certain ways of being (identities) over others, Nelson argued that using such pedagogies would help to push back against marginalizing discourses that render some lives, particularly LGBTQ+ lives, invisible. Furthermore, she argued that deploying queer theory as part of our teaching practice would allow for the creation of inclusive and critical educational spaces.

In the introduction to the *Journal of Language, Identity, and Education* special issue on LGBTQ+ considerations in language teaching, Nelson (2006) would go on to argue that there was the need to refigure the language classroom as a 'multisexual space' (2). That is, that the individuals that make up the English language classroom are just as diverse in their sexual identities and gender expressions as individuals in the wider world. She maintained, and I believe rightfully so, that acknowledging and creating inclusive space for students' sexual and gender identities in class can permit us to resist normative social discourses that view heterosexuality, and particularly monogamous, reproductive heterosexuality, as the only valued and permissible sexual identity in most modern societies (see Duggan 2002; Motschenbacher 2010, 2011b). Taking the time to purposefully create this space matters because when we teach language, we are also teaching aspects of culture and this is, largely, inescapable (see Kramsch 2004). Moreover, in our teaching we are showing our students the realms of possibility of living, being, acting, and communicating in and with cultural and social others (see Kanno 2003; Kanno and Norton 2003).

To create this environment, Nelson began outlining an inquiry-based, queer theory-informed pedagogical approach (Nelson 2002, 2006, 2009). In this approach, the primary focus is on interrogating the taken-for-granted state of affairs—the seeming dominance of heteronormative discourse as evidenced in part through curricular materials—by considering how sexuality figures into everyday life and how it is constructed and maintained by various social agents (e.g. family, schools, religion, entertainment, etc.). Through this targeted focus on sexuality—as a fact of life rather than an intimate act—we can critically examine how some sexual identities are cast as less than, or deficient to, others and how these positions are maintained through a variety of social and cultural forces. Moreover, because of queer inquiry's focus on the facts of identity instead of just the acts that constitute it, queer inquiry can serve as a vehicle to drive further critical inquiry about all identities in the classroom. It can be extended, for example, to investigate the so-called native/non-native speaker divide to show how different discourses of power over and power under work to maintain privileged and marginalized positions. It is from this starting point that much of the later work in queer TESOL/lavender ALx has sought to provide additional justifications for queering the classroom, as discussed below.

The Current State of Queer TESOL

The eight and a half years from 2010 to early 2019 have given rise to a continued explosion in research and scholarship on LGBTQ+ issues in TESOL and ELT. Studies have covered curricular considerations, teacher attitudes and training, programme development, and student identities and reactions to queered classrooms. This section will bring you up to speed, rather quickly, on the current state of queer TESOL before discussing some rather significant gaps in current disciplinary knowledge—one of which this book seeks to address. Namely, the lack of many practitioner-friendly recommendations for queering the English language classroom.

Curricular Issues in Queer TESOL

Curricular considerations are foundational to the act of queering TESOL. Granted some may feel that they do not warrant extensive consideration—especially it comes to discussing the curricular materials that we use every day in our classes (E. Russell, personal communication, 12 February 2015). However, the curriculum that our students encounter, and which we as teachers often use to structure our teaching and professional development, can have profound impacts not just on language education, but also on students' emergent views of the target culture and of their own identities in it (Ball and Feiman-Menser 1988; Grossman and Thompson 2008; Rhodes and Coda 2017; Pawelczyk, Pakuła, and Sunderland 2014). Given this importance, curricular concerns have received considerable attention of late.

For example in some of my first forays into the field, I examined a sample of 45 ESL reading texts (e.g. extensive readers, graduated novellas, etc.) and textbooks (i.e. mainline, structured, instructional texts) from 2000 to 2015 to uncover the degree to which they reflected a heteronormative worldview and if there had been any change over time (Paiz 2015a). What I found was that the sample, which largely came from commercial publishers and imprints with considerable market share, reflected a wildly heteronormative worldview. That is, very few of the texts or textbooks introduced, or even made room to engage with, sexual identities beyond monogamous, reproductive, heterosexual ones. Myself and others have identified that this is problematic because of the negative example that it sets for students about the valued ways of being in the target culture and because of the artificially constraining influence that texts and textbooks have on early-service teachers who use them to help with lesson and activity planning (see also Merse 2015; Rhodes and Coda 2017; Paiz 2015a, 2018).

Rhodes and Coda (2017), in their examination of teacher's attitudes towards and curriculum planning around the (non-)inclusion of LGBTQ+ content in their classes, found that the lack of commercially available, LGBTQ+-inclusive materials was viewed by many participants a serious constraint. Teachers in their sample felt that commercial curricular materials carried with them a certain ethos that resonated with other institutional stakeholders—administrators, peers, parents, and students. That is, students were willing to accept the commercially available materials as somehow more legitimate for educational purposes than authentic or teacher-constructed texts (ibid.: 102). While this fact creates certain challenges, many researchers have recommended that teachers find ways to use heteronormative texts as a starting point by using a queer theory, or queer inquiry, informed approach to trouble the texts for the students (see Gray 2013; Merse 2015; Paiz 2015a, 2018). Merse (2015), for example, suggested using lessons on family and relationships as a springboard for queer inquiry-based lessons, with the teacher bringing in alternative examples of non-nuclear and non-heteronormative families (see also Paiz 2015a). However, as I have elsewhere pointed out this is still a problematic approach because of the burden that it may place on early-service teachers and teachers that are working in what have been called 'frigid' environments—those environments that are hostile to the inclusion of non-normative viewpoints (Paiz 2018; Pawelczyk, Pakuła, and Sunderland 2014; Zach, Mannheim, and Alfano 2010). Moreover, students may view the textbook as the logical organizer for the course, around which activities are organized, and from which valid answers should be constructed (Pawelczyk, Pakuła, and Sunderland 2014).

Teacher Attitudes and Teacher Training

In her review of recent trends in Queer TESOL and Lavender ALx, Helen Saunston (2017) drew attention to the need to adequately train teachers to actively create inclusive educational spaces, with an eye towards creating visibility and inclusion of LGBTQ+ peoples and stories. She tied her recommendations to a report on US school environments and how they handled LGBTQ+ issues that had been released by GLSEN, a major, US-based advocacy group that investigates and spearheads policy change targeted at LGBTQ+ equity and inclusion. In that report, GLSEN (2011) found that over 80% of US LGBTQ+-identified students had reported being bullied or marginalized because of their sexual identities, perceived or actual. In the vast majority of cases, about 90%, the teacher did little to nothing to intervene on the affected students' behalf. Zach, Mannheim, and Alfano (2010: 102) identified 'four archetypes' of response when teachers were faced with homophobic acts in school settings: *avoiders*, who will seek to sidestep any discussion of LGBTQ+ issues in the classroom, even when homophobic acts occur; *confronters*, who will seek to actively counter homophobia when and where they see it; *integrators* who will actively queer the classroom in the manner that I advocate for in this book; and, *hesitators*, who feel the need to address homophobia but that they lacked the proper tools to do (ibid.: 103–105). This state of affairs, as Saunston (2017) pointed out, necessarily begs the following questions: Why aren't teachers intervening when LGBTQ+ students feel marginalized or physically threatened at schools? And, why aren't they working to create safe, equitable, and inclusive classroom environments? To answer these questions, we must first look at teachers' attitudes towards LGBTQ+ content, their place in the curriculum, and their role in helping to scaffold an inclusive learning environment. We must then turn our enquiring towards how we go about preparing new EL teachers to enter service.

Teacher's Attitudes Towards LGBTQ+ Issues

Let us turn our attention to the first question, which deals with teacher's attitudes towards LGBTQ+ issues in the English language classroom. Helpful in answering this question is looking to two, recent, small-scale surveys focusing on US-based adult and college ELT professionals (Kaiser 2017; Rhodes and Coda 2017), and one large-scale study focusing on ELT professionals that teach adult learners in the UK (MacDonald, El-Metoui, Baynham, and Gray 2014).

Rhodes and Coda (2017) surveyed 26 adult ESOL teachers working at US-based higher education institutions. Their survey was designed to elicit a variety of responses about teachers' attitudes towards creating LGBTQ+ inclusive classrooms. Their findings, however, showed that there were a range of attitudes and beliefs—about their students, local contexts, and institutional settings—that influenced whether or not they would take steps to queer their classroom practice actively. For example, they found that many teachers reported being open to including queer themes and content, but that the relative paucity of available materials made this difficult (ibid.: 102), and that institutional constraints, rather actually present or not, negatively impacted teachers' willingness to tackle LGBTQ+ topics. For example, one respondent reported that they would be happy to discuss LGBTQ+ issues in class as long as there were no students who were members of the clergy because they could, 'count on their perspectives being homophobic' (ibid.). Seeing this as an insurmountable challenge, the teacher in this case chose to gloss over queer topics altogether. Concerns about cultural appropriateness and responses from religious students were common themes among respondents in the sample as they sought to justify their disinclination to include of LGBTQ+ topics in the classroom. Rhodes and Coda also found that a teachers' perception of a lack of institutional support for queering the classroom also negatively impacted their motivation to create classrooms that considered sexual identity as part of an array of issues that needed to be addressed in inclusive classrooms.

Kaiser (2017) conducted targeted interviews with four adult ESOL teachers to come to understand their views on LGBTQ+ issues in the classroom and towards queering their classroom spaces. The teachers in his sample reported a variety of reasons for desiring to queer their practice, chief among them was a desire to help their institutions achieve their stated diversity, equity, and inclusion goals as outlined in various mission/vision statements. The participants in this study reported that they saw the failure to queer the classroom as the tacit endorsement of social stigmas about sexuality that could become internalized in classroom discourses which, in turn, could lead to their replication in the students' worldviews or views of the target culture (ibid.: 11). Despite the teachers' desire to queer their educational practice, many respondents reported that they felt unable to do so, citing concerns about the different cultural starting points for their students—especially if the student came from a traditionally more conservative cultural group (ibid.: 13). So, teachers' desires not to alienate students by spending time discussing so-called 'taboo topics' in the classroom was a chief attitude driving them to disengagement with LGBTQ+ topics altogether.

Turning to one of the largest surveys of practitioner attitudes ($n = 107$), MacDonald, El-Metoui, Baynham, and Gray (2014) identified four major attitudes of adult ESOL teachers. Briefly, those attitudes were: (1) a lack of awareness, (2) a desire not to intrude on students' private lives, (3) a view that tolerance is already addressed through more general curricular content, and (4) a belief that classrooms must engage with difficult topics—such as race, gender, and sexuality—through critical pedagogy. The first attitude, which MacDonald and colleagues labelled as 'it had never crossed my mind' (ibid.: 8), speaks to how LGBTQ+ issues may be ignored completely in ELT because they are not included in mainstream curricular materials and or institutional curriculum planning. Because of invisibility at these higher levels, they often do not rise to the surface of ELT practitioners' awareness as they engage in teaching. Instead, many wait for queer topics to come up naturally in classes, a tactic that is problematic because only a quarter of respondents reported that this happened (ibid.: 9). The second attitude that the researchers encountered in their sample was that sexuality and sexual identity are private matters. Despite holding this belief, the respondents reported being willing to tackle other, more visible, critical issues like racial discrimination. What is interesting is that when interviewed, some respondents that held this view reported that they were more concerned with their ability to respond adequately to heteronormative and homophobic attitudes in class. Wanting to avoid this possible disruption to class harmony, these practitioners would seek to avoid engagement with LGBTQ+ topics out of fears that to engage would open the door to the aforementioned negative attitudes from their students. They also cited their lack of knowledge as another reason to avoid engaging with LGBTQ+ content and to treat sexual identity and sexuality as private matters (ibid.: 10). The third attitude was that LGBTQ+ inclusion should be viewed no differently from lessons that targeted diversity, inclusion and tolerance more broadly. Teachers who held this attitude saw no need to differentiate between the various identity-based arguments for tolerance and inclusion (ibid.: 11). This approach is troubling, however, as it can continue to reinforce discourses of invisibility around queer lives and the challenges faced by members of the LGBTQ+ community around the globe. The final attitude was that we must take active steps to queer ELT through the purposeful deployment of queer theory into our teaching philosophies and pedagogies. Of the respondents to MacDonald et al.'s surveys, many reported using the critical framework advanced by Paulo Freire (1972) as one way to interrogate social identities and the discourses that maintain them. The group of teachers holding the most progressive of attitudes towards the inclusion of LGBTQ+-aware pedagogies, however, seemed to be in the minority.

Teacher Education

Two themes recur in this examination of teachers' attitudes towards including LGBTQ+ content in ELT classroom—a concern about injecting LGBTQ+-focused discussion into environments that they perceive to be unwelcoming to them (see Kaiser 2017; Rhodes and Coda 2017; Zack, Mannheim, and Alfano 2010) and a sense of a lack of proper preparation and institutional support (see Kaiser 2017; MacDonald, El-Metoui, Baynham, and Gray 2014; Rhodes and Coda 2017). Both of these themes are very closely related to issues of inclusive and critical teacher preparation, to which I would now like to focus our attention. Casting additional light on the impacts that these areas can have on new and early-service teachers can help us to understand why change needs to occur in teacher education and preparation programmes and how work like that carried out in this book can help us, as a discipline, to move the needle.

There have been very few studies done that have examined how teacher education might equip pre- and early-service teachers to queer the English language classroom. In earlier work, for example, I have discussed the systemic lack of LGBTQ+-focused training that many students in MA and PhD TESOL/TESL/Second Language Studies receive (Paiz 2018). In this conceptual piece, I conducted a quick and dirty survey of 17 graduate ESL programmes and their publically available course descriptions and syllabi. The findings indicated that only four of these programmes had any explicit mention of the possible connections between sexuality and language teaching (ibid.: 8). A response to this might be that graduate students can work to queer their own graduate training by bringing in LGBTQ+-focused research articles for in-class discussion. However, Maritz and Prinsloo (2015) correctly point out that the other affective and cognitive demands that programmes place on their graduate students mean that the students are often unable to reflect on their in-process professionalization and may be unwilling to challenge the heteronormative discourses that they may see as pervading their institutional and disciplinary contexts. Because of this state, there is a genuine need for programmes that are preparing teachers and future teacher educators to address issues of LGBTQ+ inclusion in their graduate seminars and workshops (see Shin and Vinogradova forthcoming).

MacDonald, El-Metoui, Baynham, and Gray (2014) echoed the recommendations for additional teacher education and training. They argued, however, that this education should be predicated on helping both LGBTQ+-identified and straight teachers make personal connections with members of the local LGBTQ+ community so that they can learn from their lived experiences through the sharing of life narratives. While this represents an important and potentially powerful first step, I have argued elsewhere that teacher trainers must go further than merely making personal connections (Paiz 2018). Rather, all teacher educators must adequately equip future teachers at all levels (primary, secondary, tertiary, adult ed, etc.) to purposefully queer their practice by carving out space for sometimes uncomfortable discussions about sexuality and language teaching and learning (see also Saunston 2018). To do this may mean including texts from the growing body of Queer TESOL and Lavender ALx in course reading lists, as well as modelling queer pedagogies.

Continuing Gaps in the Disciplinary Knowledge

There will always be room for growth and development in fields that are related to education, human development, and communication. That is just the nature of the work in the social sciences. There will be more that we can and should know to improve our theorizing, which in turn should be focused on informing good practice. However, there are five significant shortcomings with current disciplinary knowledge about LGBTQ+ issues in ELT that I will present to you here. They are: (1) the continued invisibility of transgender lives and issues; (2) a potential homonormative bias in current work; (3) an absences of voices from the students about how they react—both positively and negatively to the queered classroom; (4) a distinct lack of programme-level investigations; and, (5) the relative lack of regularly accessible, immediately actionable, pedagogical recommendations for queering ELT.

Transgender Invisibility in ELT

Perhaps the most disturbing gap in currently disciplinary knowledge about LGBTQ+ issues is related to transgender concerns. The almost complete omission of trans lives in the ELT literature is disturbing for two reasons. First, in North America, there has been increased attention to transgender issues in broader society. State-level legislative bodies in the United States have worked diligently to advance a spate of transphobic 'bathroom' bills that would require transgender individuals to use the bathroom that corresponds to their biological sex/gender assigned at birth (Esseks 2016). There has been a general trend upwards in violence against trans-identified individuals—note that this includes an increase in the reported murders of transgender people in the United States (Human Rights Campaign 2017). I begin with these negatives because they highlight the challenges faced by transgender people more generally; and, these are challenges that our transgender language learners will face—on top of being a marginalized part of an already marginalized community (Tulsan 2014; Weiss 2004). There has also been a marked increase in the number of visibly trans-identified characters in American TV shows like *Modern Family* (ABC), *Transparent* (Amazon), and *Orange is the New Black* (Netflix), suggesting that popular media is tapping into a more significant moment in the US cultural discourse on gender and sexuality. The continued marginalization and legislation of the transgender community, however, speaks to a need to push back against trans invisibility in ELT. In order to prepare our students—no matter their sexual identity or gender identity—to engage in respectful dialogue about trans issues, we must increase what we as a discipline know about trans educators and learners and their unique needs and insights.

I acknowledge that it may be challenging to work with marginalized populations in a research context, in part because of the importance of building relationships with research participants that are members of these communities. This challenge alone, however, is not a good enough excuse for how little Queer TESOL and Lavender ALx can tell us about how trans issues might influence language teaching, learning, and acquisition. Indeed, there is a single article that comes to mind that addresses these issues outright, Hahnthi Nguyen and Lajlim Yang's (2015) 'A Queer Learner's Identity Positioning in Second Language Classroom Discourse'. This article highlights the unique issues faced by transgender language learners even in the most inclusive of classroom spaces. Nguyen and Yang (2015) explored the classroom language learning experiences of Han, a transgender woman, and how classroom discourses positioned her in the educational space. They found that Han would often use humour to play with and to resist the gender and sexuality positionings that broader classroom discourses might try to enforce upon her. The researchers also found that Han would often push back against normative classroom practices, while also positioning herself as an effective language learner outside of the confines of the classroom space.

While Nguyen and Yang (2015) may provide a good model of respectfully reporting and conducting inquiry with/about the transgender community, there is still a great deal that the field of TESOL does not know about the needs and experiences of this student population. This lack of awareness is an issue that the field needs to immediately redress by making our disciplinary spaces more trans-inclusive and by actively pursuing trans issues as part of our research agenda (see Güney 2019). Doing so will allow ELT professionals to build more inclusive and equitable classroom spaces, and it will allow the discipline to avoid the second shortcoming in current disciplinary understandings, a potentially nascent homonormativity that is slowly creeping into our work.

An Emerging Homonormativity?

There have certainly been considerable strides in the past two decades to create more inclusive classrooms. These efforts have been grounded in frameworks like Ryuko Kubota and Angel Lin's (2006) critical race theory for TESOL and Bonny Norton and Anita Pavlenko's (2004) work interfacing gender theory with ELT. More recently, there has been an increased focus on including sexual identity, gender identity, and gender expression into critical pedagogies in TESOL (Saunston 2017). However, after spending the past five years doing research and scholarship in this area, and after reading scores of books and journal articles about the topic, I am noticing a potentially troubling emerging trend in the field, of which even some of my early work is occasionally guilty of perpetuating.

Specifically, I cannot help but wonder if we are not hurtling towards what Lisa Duggan (2002) would identify and an emerging *homonormativity*. That is, in our efforts to foster inclusive classroom spaces, are we valuing only specific homosexual identities? Perhaps, even favouring those that are most recognisable to us because of their similarity to valued heterosexual ones? Looking closely at much of the research, it seems that we may very well be. For starters, there is the almost systemic deletion of transgender lives in the literature and in scholars' and researchers' recommendations for queering the classroom (cf. Nguyen and Yang 2015 versus Rhodes and Coda 2017). Moreover, there is almost no mention of bisexual identities in the literature beyond including the 'B' in the various forms of the acronyms that are used as shorthand to reference an allegedly united community of sexual minorities (LGBT, GLBT, LGBQ, etc.). Finally, many of the recommendations for sources to turn to in order to help queer the classroom typically represent only homosexual lives that mirror their valued heterosexual counterparts. In my earlier work, I have suggested using shows like *The Fosters* or *Modern Family* to help inject LGBTQ+ content into the classroom, a message echoed by many others (see Merse 2014; Paiz 2015a). This approach, and the homonormativity that it advances, risks silencing those students whose sexual identity or gender expression do not conform to the new normal of the monogamous, lesbian or gay nuclear family.

Missing Student Voices

Much of the previous research has included some consideration of students' motivations to discuss LGBTQ+ topics (e.g. Moita-Lopes 2006), as well as discussions on how students' sexual identities can influence language learning and teaching (e.g. Moore 2013, 2016). What is largely missing, however, is any discussion that represents students' perspectives on how to carry out the work of queering the classroom, or their reactions to queered classroom spaces. This line of investigation is important because of the key role that students play as stakeholders in the language learning process. Work that I have completed with one of my former students, a Chinese ESL student at New York University (NYU) – Shanghai, provides one model for representing students' voices in this discussion (Paiz and Zhu 2018).

In 'Queering ESL Teaching: A Teacher's Decision and a Student's Response', my student and I took a dialogic approach to explore what happens when teachers decide to queer their educational practice. I began by outlining my rationale for queering the classroom and summarizing the steps I took as I attempted to introduce queer themes and perspectives in a recurring humanities seminar that I taught for NYU Shanghai, *Language, Identity, and World Englishes*. My co-author and former student then added to the article by explaining their thoughts and reactions to the queered classroom. This work is beneficial because it provides direct access to student voices. Moreover, it casts light on as to yet underexplored areas of Queer TESOL and Lavender ALx by showing us how our students are reacting to LGBTQ+-inclusive educational spaces. This perspective is critical if we are to continue advancing queer pedagogies that truly meet students' needs and expectations. The work begun by my former student and I can be expanded on by using larger sample sizes and by including voices from students that are resistant to seeing LGBTQ+-affirmatory pedagogies being deployed in classrooms.

Programme-Level Investigations

Programme development is another critical area that we need to consider as we seek to create inclusive and equitable educational spaces for sexual minority students. It is an area that matters because decisions and policies at the program level can have profound impacts on the pedagogical options that may be available to teachers (see Adler-Kassner 2008; Christison and Murray 2009; Richards 2001). Moreover, programmatic decisions can contribute to institutional cultures that advantage heteronormative attitudes and classroom practices (Merse 2017). That being said, programme design and policy remain a neglected area of research and scholarship in Queer TESOL and Lavender ALx.

Indeed, one could argue that programmatic issues are always already part of the equation when scholars like Motschenbacher (2011b) discuss heteronormativity as being endemic in many fields of linguistics; or, when Gray (2013) and myself address issues of textbook design (Paiz 2015a); or, in any of the other cases discussed in this chapter up to this point. However, because of the importance of programmatic decisions and leadership on the institutional culture and on teachers' attitudes towards their work in the local context, it deserves its own, extensive examination. Also, carrying out this work can address another issue that I feel is problematic in our field. Namely, the persistent devaluing of administrative work. As Rose and Weiser (2002) discuss in their article on administrative work in writing programmes (WPA), administration is a unique form of intellectual labour—one that requires the leveraging of emotional, disciplinary, fiscal, and leadership knowledge bases to help a programme achieve its stated mission. Given the intellectual complexity of administrative labour, this means that we should treat administration and programmatic issues in ELT as seriously as any of the other issues in our collective research agenda.

Ashley Moore's (2016) 'Inclusion and Exclusion: A Case Study of an English Class for LGBT Learners' offers a look at an English class designed around the needs of LGBTQ+ language learners in Japan. Moreover, it is also one of the few pieces that speak more directly to some of the programmatic issues in queering the English language classroom. In this article, Moore gives voice to the language learners' concerns about traditional language classes, stating that they found them to be silencing and othering spaces. The student-participants felt that in more conventional language programmes, there was little chance of discussing LGBTQ+ topics and that performing an out LGBTQ+ identity could be seen as problematic, leading to stigmatization and ostracization by their peers or teachers. The students reported feeling that more traditional programmes created an ethos of exclusion for sexual minorities.

Moore (2016) then contrasts this with an English language class that was part of a broader LGBT programme at a non-governmental organization (NGO). In the course for LGBT leaners, Moore points to some programme design decisions that can lead to more inclusive spaces. First, he draws our attention to the need to focus on relationship building in inclusive programme design. To help students to feel more comfortable engaging with critical issues of sexual literacy and identity, we must first focus on building nurturing and welcoming relationships between the students, their peers, their teachers, and the programme administrators. Without a healthy relationship between these various stakeholders, students may feel concern over whether or not their participation will be treated as legitimate by their institutionally significant others. Second, Moore (ibid.) highlights the needs for the programme to take an open orientation to matters of sexual identity. In part, this means creating spaces where students and teachers can engage in frank discussions about these issues. Also, it points to the need for teachers to avoid essentializing or reductive views of sexual identity or sexual minority communities. To avoid doing so means moving away from the notion of a monolithic global 'gayness' to embracing the varied ways that sexual identities are expressed and maintained in local contexts and sub-cultures.

Practitioner-Friendly Pedagogical Recommendations

Having drawn our attention to the programme-level blind spot, I would now like to pull our focus to the level of the individual. Despite considerable research having been conducted on LGBTQ+ issues in ELT over the past twenty years, there is still a relative dearth of practitioner-friendly pedagogical recommendations. I have been presenting on LGBTQ+ issues in ELT and World Englishes at conferences across the United States and parts of the People's Republic of China since 2013. In that time, I have been approached by practitioners that are at the conference as part of their school's continuing professional development requirements and who have raised very important questions, such as, 'What you said is great and all, but what I am supposed to do with it?; What can I do to make my classroom more inclusive of sexual minority students?; What does a queered classroom actually look like?' This suggests to me, that despite my own best efforts, and that of many other researchers in Queer TESOL and Lavender ALx, there is still a genuine need to provide practitioners with a practical toolkit for them to queer their practice. Detailing one such framework is the primary goal of this book. To help facilitate this work, I will be building on Cynthia Nelson's (2006, 2009) Queer Inquiry as that basis for a range of pedagogical approaches, which I will label as queer inquiry-based pedagogies.

Moving Towards Queer Pedagogies

The remainder of this book will focus on helping practitioners, at any stage in their professional development, find actionable ways to queer their practice by constructing their own queer inquiry-based pedagogy. Moreover, it will provide teacher educators with a starting point for preparing future educators to engage in critical practice by creating educational spaces that are accessible to LGBTQ+ individuals. To do this, I will be using Cynthia Nelson's (2006, 2009) notion of *Queer Inquiry* to drive educational practices that speak to matters of sexual identity and diversity, equity, and inclusion. Central to this notion is that inclusive classroom spaces must equip students with the tools for critical thinking and engagement that allows them to make sense of how their social settings (re)create and police identities that have more or less value in the local context. This approach is useful because it allows us to queer the classroom in culturally responsive ways and in diverse institutional and national contexts. That is, the queer pedagogies advocated for in this book are designed to be responsive to teachers' local settings in a way that increases the likelihood that the queered classroom might resonate with students and, at least in the context of the classroom, give those in marginalized positions a voice with which to speak truth to power (Healy and Mullholland 2012).

Another cornerstone of queer inquiry-based pedagogies is that they work to create spaces where marginalized identities are adequately represented in educational planning and curricular materials. While much of my focus will be on sexual identity, we must acknowledge that sexual identity does not become salient for individuals in isolation. Instead, it is always already at the intersection of other identities—religious, political, racial, ethnic, gender, etc.—at which sexualities gain nuanced relevance for individuals. That is, the intersection of race and sexuality means that the lived experiences and concerns of a Latinx, lesbian who is a naturalized citizen of the United States are different from those of an American-born Chinese, transgender, lesbian. This means that we must critically think of how our curricular materials, even ones that engage with sexual identity topics, reify dominant discourses about identities—creating new value around some identities (e.g. White, able-bodied, cisgender gay male) while continuing to marginalize others (e.g. straight-identified, transgender, person of colour with a physical disability).

A final major cornerstone of the pedagogy approaches that I advocate for here is the need to find room for local voices—of students, teachers, administrators, community members, etc.—in the queered classroom. This may take the form of creating space for students to, if comfortable, lead discussions. Alternatively, it could mean finding ways to empower teacher-leaders to help advance their colleagues' professional development in matters related to LGBTQ+ diversity and inclusion. Or, it may mean, as Curran (2006) did, finding space in classroom assignments and curricular materials for students to engage with content based on the lived experiences of members of the local LGBTQ+ community.

Conclusion

Before digging into the 'meat' of this book and the queer-informed pedagogies for which it advocates, I want to conclude this chapter by first providing you with what I, see as the key takeaways from this protracted introduction to queer TESOL and lavender ALx. I then want to invite you to engage in some reflection that you will then attempt to make actionable as you work through the remainder of this book—this to me, reflection *plus* action, is how we become *reflexive educators.* These kinds of teachers are ones that are best equipped to advocate for their students and their colleagues, while also beginning to serve as teacher-leaders in their institutional context.

Key Takeaways

Having read this chapter, or skipped to this point, here are the crucial points that you should carry forward with you as you read through the rest of this book.

- Engaging with queer issues and sexual literacy concerns in the language classroom is a worthwhile endeavour because the visibility that it brings to LGBTQ+ lives can help to facilitate an educational environment that supports language learning and emerging L2 identities.
- Moreover, creating visibility around LGBTQ+ lives in the English language classrooms can help to interrogate normative

social discourses. This act can help students to understand better how their identities as students, language learners/users, etc. are situated in cultural discourses that begin to frame more and less accepted ways of living, being, and acting in their ecosocial context.

- Creating LGBTQ+-inclusive English language classrooms requires turning a critical eye towards the materials that we choose to deploy in our classrooms. Given that most commercially available materials reflect a strong heteronormative bias, educators must find ways to trouble these materials for students to lay bare the ways that they render some lives as *less than* others.
- Finding ways to queer the classroom that are grounded in the local context can help educators to be culturally responsive in their efforts. Moreover, including local queer voices can also help to render these lives visible—further troubling normative discourses.

Reflexive Praxis Prompt

A central act of being an effective educator is to reflect critically on our practice (Edge 2011). Beyond merely making time to reflect on what we do in our classrooms—what is working (best practices) and what is not (better practices)—we must also seek ways to turn our reflections into plans that will drive improvements in our practice. That is, effective educators are *reflexive educators* (ibid.). To aid the reader in their reflexive practice, each chapter of this book will include a few questions to help you apply the material from the chapter to your practice.

- What motivates you to want to queer your educational/professional praxis? Was there an event in your training, institutional life, or classroom that has encouraged you to seek ways to make your classroom more inclusive of sexual minorities?
- What challenges—personal, professional, institutional, and material—will likely create issues as you attempt to queer your

practice? How will you overcome them? What can you do to mitigate these challenges? Who can you partner with to assist you in your efforts?

- What biases, both positive and negative, might you have regarding sexual literacy, diversity, and inclusion that cause issues as you attempt to queer your practice?
- What do you currently know about LGBTQ+ lives and language in your local community? How might this help you as you attempt to queer your classroom practice? What do you still need to know? Whom can you partner with to fill in gaps in your current knowledge?

2

Queer Inquiry as Pedagogy

AT A GLANCE

Introduction

The previous chapter discussed the past and current trends in Queer TESOL and Lavender ALx. This chapter will begin the work of taking the foundation from Chapter 1 and outlining a pedagogical approach that is based on Nelson's (2006, 2009) queer inquiry. This description will be aimed at allowing the reader to understand how queer inquiry can be applied to educational practice at both the classroom and the curricular levels. Moreover, this description is one that should allow the practitioner, or the teacher educator, to feel comfortable introducing others to a queer inquiry-based pedagogical framework. Now, I must take a moment to acknowledge that some will take issue with any attempt to outline queer pedagogy/ies. Stacy Waite in *Teaching Queer: Radical Possibilities for Writing and Knowing* goes so far as to call the delineation of a queer pedagogy paradoxical in both definition and practice (Waite 2017: 36) because the theoretical construct of *queer* is predicated on fluidity and flexibility—on resisting normative forces (see Bristow 2011; Jagose 1997; Sullivan 2003). While I agree, in part, with this assertion, I also know that we must, even temporarily, pin down critical terms and approaches in order to effect meaningful change that moves beyond the profession and the professional and into the educational and personal worlds of our students. Therefore, however, the pedagogy that I will be outlining throughout this chapter should be seen as but one approach to understanding queer inquiry-based pedagogy. I would argue, as would many of my colleagues, that there are multiple ways to queer the classroom. Indeed, one of the hallmarks of the pedagogical approach that I will discuss throughout this chapter is that it is customizable to meet local needs and constraints. In seeking to help practitioners queer the classroom, this book is not handing down directives but is highlighting possibilities—which are multiple, context-driven, and emergent in nature.

After introducing the queer inquiry-based pedagogy, this chapter will then move to discuss the contextual threats and opportunities that exist regarding any queer inquiry-driven pedagogy. Then, it will discuss how to address a variety of contextual concerns by managing expectations and turning resistance to LGBTQ+ inclusion into a teaching opportunity. Once that is completed, the chapter will conclude with a reflexive prompt to guide the reader as they consider how to integrate the ideas of this chapter into their practice.

Issues and Starting Points

To help frame the discussion of the queer inquiry-based pedagogy for which I wish to advocate, I begin by continuing the discussion of the issues that this pedagogical approach seeks to lay bare for the students and the educator. After that, I will discuss the philosophical starting point for this pedagogical approach, which will serve as a touchstone as you seek to queer your practice and to build a queered pedagogy that works for you and your local context.

Issues on which Queer Inquiry-Based Pedagogies Can Shed Light

As discussed in Chapter 1, issues of sexual literacy and sexual identity's impact on language acquisition, learning, and teaching have come under increasing scrutiny in recent years.[1] Its continued focus in the modernization of the field is further evidenced by the relative health of the International LGBTQ Forum of TESOL International Association, the recent formation of a dedicated interest section of the Linguistic Society of America (2018), and the organization of a special colloquium on LGBTQ+ issues at the 2018 meeting of the American Association For Applied Linguistics (Coda 2018b). This continued interest is driven, in part, by the myriad of issues that a queer inquiry-based pedagogy can begin to address. As Coda (2018b) and Saunston (2018) have correctly pointed out, queered pedagogical approaches like the one advanced below can reinforce liberatory approaches to education that seek to address social justice issues in the language classroom.

Regulation and Value of Sexuality and Identity

One of the primary issues that a queer inquiry-based pedagogy can address is that of how sexuality, specifically, and identities, more generally, come to be regulated and valued in society. Coming to a better understanding of how social value is created and how societal power structures regulate our lives is an essential aspect of any critically informed pedagogy, and it is an issue with which the critical educator should be trained to engage. It is an important area because, as Yang (2012: 54) correctly stated, 'a learner whose identity does not fit within the constructs of a particular community or classroom may not be fully engaged and learning within the particular group'. This admonition has direct implications for student investment in formalized language learning activities and with how well they may integrate with the broader educational community that makes up their cohort, programme, or school (see Cahnmann-Taylor and Coda 2018; Saunston 2018; Yang 2012). Moreover, lowered investment can lead to students being cast as deficient learners by educators and administrators because of their ambivalence, if not outright resistance towards, formalized language learning environments (see A. Ibrahim 1999).

Therefore, deploying pedagogies that encourage learners to understand how identity is constructed, performed, and regulated in social groups—of which the classroom and the school is certainly one—can be helpful in getting students to think critically about their place in the educational institution and how they, and others, use language to enact, understand, and respond to their own subject positions and those of others. Moreover, it can help learners *and* educators alike to question the ways that dominant social discourses perform regulatory functions through creating normalizing social forces, which I would like to turn our attention towards next.

Critical Engagement with Normativity and Its Impacts

Another benefit of queer inquiry-based pedagogy is that it encourages students and teachers to confront the influence of normative social discourses on our lives. By creating space for students to engage, explicitly and at length, with issues of identity and language, queer inquiry-based pedagogies lay bare the ways that in- and out-groups are created, maintained, and regulated in society. So, here, it becomes vital to consider intersections between gender, sexuality, and language learning. For example, by being critically aware, a teacher can begin to question intersections between gender and sexuality and how normative discourses may predispose them to respond to students in certain ways. Returning to an example from earlier, Liddicoat (2009) showed how the uncritical, or at least busy and therefore myopically focused, educator could inadvertently marginalize sexual minority students by not considering lived gender/sexual identity performance when evaluating student responses. That is, we run the risk of casting gender/sexual minority students as poor language learners when we follow our lesson plans, textbooks, or internalized scripts too closely.

For our students, failure to critically engage with normative social discourses about gender, sexuality, and language learning can lead to disengagement from formalized language learning or from activities that aid in second language acquisition (SLA). Turning again to the work of Anthony Liddicoat (2018) can provide insights into what is at risk when we, as educators, administrators, and curriculum planners, do not consider the potential negative impacts of normative social discourses. Speaking of his experiences as a Spanish as a foreign language instructor in Australia and the UK, he showed how many male students view language learning as an activity in which female students are more likely to succeed. This view, he argued, is maintained by dominant social discourses that set up girls and young women as better language learners and communicators than boys and young men. This leads to successful male language learners being marked as either atypical of their gender or differently othered in ways that call their masculinities into question, such as through attacking their perceived or actual sexual identity. Because of this, male students may feel a tacit social pressure to under-perform, or to remain silent, in the language classroom—if they do not opt out of advanced language learning altogether (see Carr and Pauwels 2006; Liddicoat 2018; Sunderland 2000a, 2000b).

Queer inquiry-based pedagogies provide tools to lay bare the impact of normative discourses in the language classroom. Moreover, they allow students and educators to find locally relevant, linguistically accessible means of challenging these discourses. Teachers using a queer-informed approach can trouble normative curricular materials and classroom practices to create classroom spaces that are welcoming to students from traditionally marginalized gender and sexuality backgrounds. Students can work together to come to better understandings of ways to respectfully engage with identities that deviate from the so-called norm—creating additional opportunity for their marginalized peers to find a voice in the classroom.

Critical Thinking Skills

Additionally, the literature has suggested that queer-inquiry based pedagogies also facilitate the acquisition and refining of critical thinking skills. Specifically, most queer-inquiry based pedagogies are designed to support students as they seek to problematize dominant social discourses and their often invisible influence on our daily lives. Following from Pennycook (2001, 2006), queer pedagogies make space for students to engage in a wilful, purposeful, and unending problematizing of what is assumed as given, natural, and true. Take, for example, the work of Ó'Móchain (2006) at the Christian women's college in Japan. He was able to encourage students to engage in thinking critically about identity and accepted ways of living and being by asking his students to engage in life narrative work—collecting life stories from community citizens. Ó'Móchain (2006) made it a point of including in the sample members of the LGBTQ+ community who were able to speak about the social pressures to hide their sexual identity or to conform to social norms. This created space for students to first be made aware of ways of life deemed to be outside the social norm. Then, he was able to encourage students to engage in critical reflection by asking students questions about the narratives that they collected and were organizing that sought to uncover how others may have marginalized these sexual minorities or how the minority participants may have co-opted dominant discourses to find a voice and position of recognition.

What is important to note here, however, is that using a queer inquiry approach alone is not enough to help students engage in and to hone their critical thinking. Instead, it is vital that the teacher take steps to actively create the opportunity to engage students' critical thinking in a dialogic and negotiated manner. While critical pedagogies may seek to equip students with certain attitudes and best practices, they do not seek to instil a specific ideological leaning. This fact means that making room for all perspectives, even those we may disagree with, is important in order to avoid groupthink or superficial critical thinking that occurs to please the teacher.

Pushing Beyond the 'Comfort Zone' to Engage with Social Justice Concerns

It is a common saying that life happens outside of one's comfort zone; and, this saying has been applied to learning in various forms as well, such as in sociocultural theories that advocate for teaching to the students' zone of proximal development (see Lantolf and Aljafreeh 1995; Vygotsky 1978) and in SLA theories that advocate for input just beyond the learners' current level (see Krashen 1985).[2] I would argue that one benefit of queer-informed pedagogies is that they push students beyond their potential comfort zones when it comes it issues of social justice and equity. As with language learning and instructed SLA, this may create the needed space for students to grapple with complex issues in a way that can affect greater understanding and the potential for change in long-standing beliefs or biases.

Recent work by Helen Saunston provides an excellent example of the potentially transformative power of queer-inquiry based pedagogies. Working in a multinational, graduate-level ESOL teacher education programme, Saunston (2018) made the decision to include research and scholarship from the fields of Queer TESOL and Lavender ALx in her course syllabus; moreover, she chose to utilise a pedagogical approach that was inspired by Nelson's (2006, 2009) queer inquiry. She reported that in both British and Mainland Chinese contexts that some of her students were initially uncomfortable with the readings and the discussions that they brought up in the classroom, with some of them chuckling nervously. However, when the readings were viewed as part of a critical framework for ESOL (Pennycook 2001, 2006), the students began to see how these readings and discussions forced them to come to terms with how sexuality and the marginalization of non-normative sexual identities played out in their local contexts. Additionally, she stated that by pushing students through momentary discomfort they reported feeling better prepared to professionally handle these issues if and when they would arise in their teaching—even if they found themselves working in a more socially conservative institutional context (Saunston 2018). While her work focused on teacher educators in multinational contexts, similar results have been shown for younger students (Moita-Lopes 2006) and students in early stages of the language learning and acquisition process (see Cahnmann-Taylor and Coda 2018; Merse 2017; Miller and Endo 2018).

Philosophical Starting Points for Queer Inquiry-Based Pedagogies

The previous chapter provided you with a contextualizing overview of LGBTQ+ issues and investigations on TESOL and applied linguistics (ALx). Here, however, I would like distil that down into what I see as the primary philosophical exigencies for selecting and building a pedagogy that allows you to queer your practice. In this section, I will be sharing the aspects of my teaching philosophy that drove me to want to queer my practice, and I will tie this to debates in the literature.

Co-constructing Knowledge about Language and the World

Following from Atkinson (2002, 2011), I believe that one part of what we do when we teach, especially in the English language classroom, is to engage in the act of co-constructing knowledge with our students about language and the ecosocial settings in which our students will encounter it—a key tenant of the sociocognitive approach to SLA. That is, in the classroom, we are not just talking about the world through course content, and we are not just engaging in learning discreet linguistic items—whether they be new lexical tokens, new syntactic patterns, and so on. Instead, we are engaged in the joint action of co-constructing our knowledge about language, language use, and its role in our ecosocial settings—that is, in our lived worlds and between our socially significant others (see also

Atkinson, Churchill, Nishino, and Okada 2007; Atkinson and Sohn 2013; Churchill 2007). Language teaching, therefore, is an act of working alongside our students to not only activate their pre-existing knowledge about language and the world but also to learn from them about their locally relevant ways of using languages to make meaning.

This act of co-constructing knowledge and meaning is a central philosophical starting point for queering the English language classroom because successfully introducing LGBTQ+ content into the classroom and helping students respectfully and meaningfully engage with these themes, requires us to accept that there are a multitude of ways of *being* LGBTQ+. Moreover, the experience of LGBTQ+ life is not the same across regional, national, and cultural borders (e.g. Khayatt 2003; Liu 2015). That is, being a cisgender, gay man in the United States for a person of colour represents a radically different set of identity options than being one in the People's Republic of China—or even in Taiwan (see Liu 2015). So, in order to better queer our practice, we must engage *with* our students and the knowledge that they bring with them to our classrooms and institutions. From this starting point, we can begin to co-construct our knowledge about LGBTQ+ lived experiences at those border zones, about their lived differences, and about how language has been used to inscribe more and less acceptable ways of being LGBTQ+ in different contexts. Then, we can take an essential step in our work of queering the classroom—troubling normalizing discourses.

Challenging Normalizing Discourses and Decreasing Stigmatization

The second philosophical starting point for queering the English language classroom is one that comes directly from the fields of Queer TESOL and Lavender ALx. Namely, it is the need to help students identify normalizing social discourses and understanding the often tacit, yet profound, effects of these social discourses on our daily lives. To achieve this outcome requires encouraging students to acquire the mindset of restive problematizing (Pennycook 2006)—of continually seeking out underlying assumptions and beliefs about the world and language and questioning them from a critical perspective. Additionally, the restive problematizing called for by queer inquiry-based pedagogies requires challenging normative discourses where we encounter them even if it does not directly impact our lives (see Nelson 2006, 2009).

While this may seem to be grounded almost entirely in social justice concerns, this restive problematizing of the norm can interface with other pedagogical and philosophical considerations. For example, students in many academic writing classes are not only working on acquiring a stronger command of the English writing system and its myriad differences from spoken English but also on acquiring a better understanding of the underlying rhetorical differences—of how to construct and maintain a reasoned, evidence-based argument. In this setting, a restive problematizing of the given, of what students assume to be true, can be very useful in helping them to construct more robust arguments that are aligned with the Aristotelian or Rogerian rhetorics that are valued in many English-dominant academic circles (see Bator 1980; Lunsford 1979). Another benefit is that instilling students with a mindset of restive problematizing that can help them to better understand the ways that normative language practices (i.e. only valuing inner-circle, native speaker English) can limit their multi-/trans-lingual expressive abilities or cast them and their local varieties of English (e.g. Indian English, Black South African English, etc.) as somehow deficient or less than (see Anderson 2018; Canagarajah 2013; Kachru and Nelson 2006).

Fostering Ownership of Learning and Critical Engagement

Teaching is probably one of the few professions where we seek to end our students' dependence on us—it is built on a sort of planned obsolescence. That is if we as educators do our job well, our students should no longer need us as teachers. Yes, we may continue as mentors, role models, professional peers, and even friends but our job as their teacher is largely over once they leave our classroom or our schools. This state means that we must do our part to ensure that students move towards increased ownership over their learning and critical engagement with their ecosocial contexts during their time with us. By helping learners to take greater agency, we can help instil in them the attitudes and habits of mind necessary to be successful lifelong learners (Knapper and Cropley 2000). A queer inquiry-based pedagogy can help foster this ownership by decentring the classroom—highlighting the value of negotiated meaning making and casting the teacher as a model of lifelong learning as they seek to learn with and from their students. Additionally, a queer inquiry-based approach can allow the teacher to model dutiful approaches to critical engagement—ones that are not predicated on power-over/power-under relationships, but on respectful engagement with others and with diverse viewpoints.

A Description of One Queer Inquiry-Based Pedagogy

Now that we have dug a little deeper into what a queer inquiry-based pedagogy can help to address in the classroom, as well as the philosophical starting points for this approach, it is time to turn our attention to a description of one such pedagogy. Understand, that this is only a description of a single approach to queering the classroom—it is far from the *only* approach. Indeed, to argue for a single approach to queering English language teaching would be against the very ideals of Queer TESOL/Lavender ALx—namely of resisting and troubling normative discourses. In the section following this one, I will discuss how you can use this description to begin building your own queer pedagogical tool kit.

In this section, I will focus on describing how I have queered my classroom practice. The approach outlined here was not one that was arrived at suddenly, or that was uncovered from existing literature in any well-formed, pre-packaged manner. Instead, it has come through my years of service as an educator in diverse contexts, through my research and scholarship into LGBTQ+ issues in TESOL, through my engagement with my local context, through with my own experiences as a cisgender, gay, male educator, and through a lot of trial and error. This discussion of my approach to queer inquiry-based pedagogy will be linked back to the issues and philosophical starting points discussed in the previous section to provide you with real-world examples of the pedagogical implications of each of these. I will then discuss how this approach changes in different classroom contexts—focusing on the teaching contexts with which I have the most experience: first-year writing, humanities seminars, and graduate professional literacy class.

Queer Inquiry-Based Pedagogy: A Look at a Personal Case

During my doctoral studies, I toyed with the idea of queering my classroom practice. At that time, however, I was still trying to get my feet under me as far as understanding the theoretical foundations and the pedagogical best practices for doing so. I will admit that I was also a bit nervous. I existed in an odd and almost contingent space, being simultaneously an early-service educator and a student—a junior professional and yet a novice. So, it wasn't really until I was a full-time faculty member that I actually worked up the courage to roll up my sleeves and start queering the classroom—in part because I had increased freedom and in part because I felt that I had reached a better understanding of the theory that drives Queer TESOL and Lavender ALx. So, this led me to the philosophical starting points addressed in the previous section. I have since been using these starting points—co-constructing knowledge with my students, challenging normative discourse, and encouraging critical ownership of learning—to guide my efforts to queer my classrooms.

I firmly believe that when we engage in the act of teaching, of creating learning opportunities for *and with* our students, we are engaging in the act of co-(re)constructing knowledge about the world that we live in, the language that we use, and the values that we place on language use and proficiency alongside our students. This view is heavily informed by Dwight Atkinson's sociocognitive approach to second language acquisition, which posits that language learning, acquisition, and use can only happen through meaningful joint action between ourselves and our socially significant others (see Atkinson 2002, 2011). This viewpoint interfaces nicely with queer inquiry-based pedagogies because it removes from the teacher the onus to be the know-it-all resource about queer matters. Paraphrasing Nelson Rodriguez and William Pinar's (2007) introduction to *Queering Straight Teachers: Discourse and Identity in Education*, it is up to all teachers, not just LGBTQ+-identified ones, to make the classroom inclusive of sexual minorities. Additionally, willingly engaging in co-construction of knowledge with our students, while potentially daunting because of the surrender of some control to the students, also addresses one of the major concerns about queering the classroom that has been voiced by straight-identified educators—namely, that they do not know enough about LGBTQ+ life to integrate queer material and voices into their classes successfully (see MacDonald, El-Metoui, Baynham, and Gray 2014).

So, my approach to queer inquiry-based pedagogy begins from a position of co-construction and joint inquiry. This means working with our students to come to a better understanding of what it means to be a member of the LGBTQ+ community in our local context and to understand respectful ways of engaging with and talking about that community. Doing so allows us to come to a better understanding of how we have seen and experienced the regulation of sexual identities in and across contexts. For example, my Chinese students and I have discovered different ontological beginnings for the regulation of sexual identities in the US and the China. In the US, LGBTQ+ sexual identities have often been legally regulated by appealing to Christian values; while in China, the State has sought to regulate sexuality through appeals to social unity and stability (see Liu 2015; Paiz, Comeau, Zhu, Zhang, and Santiano 2018).

Another essential objective of any queer inquiry-based pedagogy is to challenge normative discourses—about sexual identity, language, and much more. For me, this means creating classroom spaces and pedagogical practices that take a scaffolded approach to this work. It begins, in many cases, by queering our discussion about language and language use. To do this work, I will often bring in readings about global variation in the English language and welcome my students to reflect with me on questions like, 'Who *owns* English?'; 'Who gets to determine what is *proper* English?'; 'What makes the so-called owners of English (frequently native speakers) so special?'; 'What do the privileged native speakers have to lose if we challenge their ownership and control over the language?'. Over time, I expose them to writing done in non-Western varieties of English (e.g. Singaporean English, Sri Lankan English, etc.) and ask them to reflect with me on how normative views of English favour the native speaker and may continually disadvantage them—the so-called non-native speakers. I then ask them to engage with me and with readings from fields like queer linguistics and World Englishes to imagine what non-normative views of language look like and what the consequences might be when those views go mainstream (e.g. B. Kachru 1990; Motschenbacher 2011a; Motschenbacher and Stegu 2013; Y. Kachru and Nelson 2006). Later in the semester, we use a similar scaffolded approach to discussing topics related directly to sexuality in our local context. I find that this approach equips students with the tools to critically engage with the idea of normativity by first thinking about it in relation to their own lives as second language learners and users of English. This approach then facilitates the discussion of normative views of sexual identity by providing a more personal touchstone to students who either are not members of the LGBTQ+ community or who do not have close friends or family that identify as such. Moreover, the use of a similar set of guiding questions means that students are prepared for the kind of intellectual labour that comes with troubling social givens.

In recent years, there have been increased calls for education to move towards a model of global citizenship education, or GCE. GCE focuses on preparing students to take ownership over their civic engagement on a global scale and to engage with nationalistic assumptions critically as they come to see themselves as global citizens (see Davies and Pike 2009; T. Ibrahim 2005; Pigozzi 2006). My approach to queer inquiry-based pedagogy seeks to encourage students to first take increasing and ever critical ownership over their learning, especially as it relates to LGBTQ+ topics and issues. I begin by telling them about my views and research as they relate to our course topics. For example, when discussing queer lives in the US and China, I make it very clear that what I say in the classroom is not the only possible viewpoint—nor is it necessarily the correct one. It is merely based on my subjective experiences as a married, cisgender, gay man and as an active researcher focusing on LGBTQ+ topics in English language education globally. So, when we are discussing family terms in a basic ESL tutorial, I include families that have single parents and same-sex parents. I then encourage my students to take time to reflect on other so-called 'non-traditional' family organizational patterns and to question why mainstream culture, in the United States at least, places so much value on the nuclear family. I make it clear that while we may discuss it further in class later, but it is up to them to go and to find out more. That is, I am merely providing them with a starting point—it is up to them to go and continue learning, to continue seeking out and constructing new knowledge about the world by synthesizing what we learned in class with their own subjective experiences and objective observations based on external source material. Moreover, I push them to question what they assume to be given and true about basic social structures and the world around them. The goal is to instil a mindset that drives them to become lifelong learners and to be able to take ownership over that process. Central to this goal is to equip them with the strategies and attitudes needed to become critical thinkers (e.g. Halpern 2013; ten Dam and Volman 2004).

Often, this requires students to accept that they will have to move outside of their comfort zones to engage with new ideas and perspectives to come to a fuller understanding of complex social and linguistic issues. To help students with this, I build into my queer pedagogy places where I model for my students how I seek out opportunities to engage with ideas that may be outside of my comfort zone. When it comes to LGBTQ+ content, I share with them frankly about my evolving understanding of gender and gender non-conformity issues and how I must purposefully seek out information about these topics and take the time to engage with them. I also work with them to uncover how their own lived experiences may create certain biases that they will have to challenge—often these biases form the foundation of their comfort zones. To do this, I talk with my students about my childhood, which was heavily steeped in socially conservative, fundamentalist Christian communities. After sharing with them some of the values and beliefs of that community, I invite them to think with me about how that might have shaped my thinking during my youth about LGBTQ+ issues—especially contemporary issues around transgender visibility and gender non-conformity. We then work on a frank discussion of how our other beliefs may shape our thinking about LGBTQ+ lives and issues before working together to try to see the topics under discussion from different perspectives.

What Can this Queer Inquiry-Based Pedagogy Look Like in Different Class Contexts?

Next, I will provide you with some examples of what the queer inquiry-based pedagogy discussed above looks like when I have used it in different types of classrooms. Note that the classes discussed in this section have taken place in both the US and the China. Also, as I am primarily a university educator, my examples come from the higher and adult education context. In the following chapters, I will bring the K-12 context more sharply into focus.

First-Year Writing

I have been teaching first-year writing courses at least part-time since 2009. And, when I first started teaching, I actively avoided LGBTQ+ issues and content in my classes—first, out of a desire to keep the class apolitical, and second, because I was not sure how to include this material in a respectful, meaningful way. However, I will never forget when one of my students during the second semester of teaching, wrote a short personal essay about reconciling their sexual and their religious identities. I was a bit surprised by the frankness of their discussion and by their skilful use of the narrative and expressive techniques that we had talked about in class. That was when I began to wonder what it might mean for LGBTQ+ students to see themselves better represented in the class and its materials.

Over time, I would come to actively attempt to queer the first-year writing courses that I would teach. In every class, the core philosophy is that of problematizing dominant discourses. This means that the focus isn't just on sexual identity, but also linguistic domination, on gender normativity, on Western bias in secondary research, and so on. My attempts to queer my teaching became most explicit and purposeful when I began teaching at New York University–Shanghai (NYU Shanghai/上海纽约大学). I would open each class by sharing what kind of research I was interested in with my students, telling them that I engage in research that looks at sexual identity and its possible influences on language learning and teaching. I would tell them that I do not share this because I want them to think as I think. Instead, I share this information to help them situate me as a professional and as their professor; I share this with them because it informs my teaching and how they will experience my classroom spaces. I repeat throughout the course that they never need to agree with me, but they must learn to disagree respectfully and to base that disagreement on something outside of themselves—all of which I will help them to do during our time together.

My first-year writing course at NYU Shanghai focused on language, literacy, and higher education. And, during the semester, I would build in readings from academic and popular sources that either included LGBTQ+ content or that somehow troubled and queered other dominant discourses. For example, as we discuss language, I include readings from Ha Jin (2012) on the use of solecisms (foreign-like expressions) when writing in English. This piece, 'In Defence of Foreignness', kicks off our semester by immediately asking students to begin thinking about what normative discourses about the English language they have encountered in their own language learning before coming to NYU Shanghai. While discussing this reading, we often encounter questions about who benefits from a normative view of the English language. That is, who can stand to reap the most political, cultural, and economic capital from control over what we consider to be right and proper English? We also end up encountering questions of what happens if we challenge this view that only American, Australian, British, or Canadian (read: inner circle) Englishes are valid and valuable. These kinds of questions, ones that seek to lay bare our unspoken assumptions about the current and correct order of the world around us are central to a pedagogy of queer inquiry—remember, it is not just about sex and sexuality. It is about uncovering and problematizing *all* normative discourses in which we are awash.

These discussions about normative views of English will inevitably lead to students expressing views that so-called non-standard (read: non-Western) Englishes are problematic because there may be intelligibility issues. At this point, I will often switch gears in my course away from academic readings and towards creative ones by bringing in works that are classified by World Englishes scholars as contact literatures. *Contact literatures* are those works that have been written by multilingual authors and set in and that focus on issues in non-English dominant contexts (Thumboo 2006). So, we will often read 'The Bridegroom', a short story by Ha Jin (2001) that focuses on a man in post-cultural revolution China that is arrested for having sexual relationships with other men. Our primary focus is on how Ha Jin uses China English to craft a narrative with increased local relevance and fidelity to the socio-historical context of which he is writing. However, the queer content of the story also leads us to apply our problematizing questions to the protagonist's predicament. We end up exploring how societal and familial expectations led to specific sexual identities being deemed more valued and valid than others. We then discuss how these expectations were maintained through language and State regulation. I then ask them to think about how the situation has changed or might be in a state of flux in modern China.

During the semester, we also applied our problematizing questions: Why is it this way? Who benefits? Who is disadvantaged? What maintains it? to questions of higher education and to doing research—as one of the primary goals of the course is to introduce students to secondary/library research and research writing at the undergraduate level. When we get to research writing and talking about citation and finding sources, I continue to make use of queer-inquiry based pedagogies. When talking about citation and building a research-based argument, I often return us to our earlier scholarly readings to examine the intellectual lineage of one of the pieces that we read. In this exercise, we examine the references that the author used to support their theoretical framework—the lens through which they analyse the world. One issue that becomes apparent to students is that much of the published literature that is cited in mainstream academic sources is (a) written in English, (b) published in mainstream journals by Western publishers, (c) utilize Western theories as their base, or some combination thereof. We then apply our problematizing questions to this situation, and I encourage students to find ways to begin to break this norm creatively. Given that many of them are writing about issues in education in the Chinese context they find ways to not only bring in Chinese language academic sources but also alternative sources like videos from *Guokr* (果壳), a Chinese site that organizes talks similar to TED talks.

The goal in the first-year writing class is one of raising awareness and of equipping students with a critical toolkit that they can carry forward with them. This objective is why the problematizing questions discussed above are returned to multiple times and applied to different domains of inquiry. Throughout the course, I am working on getting students comfortable with coming to see the normalizing discourses around them, and how they influence their daily lives and the choices that they make about language and education. Towards the end of the semester, we move towards ways of actively troubling (queering) those norms by relying more on alternative ways of knowing, being, thinking, and speaking about the world around us.

Undergraduate Core Curriculum

During my time at NYU Shanghai, I was asked to teach a humanities seminar in our core curriculum. The design of this course was left entirely to my discretion, so I decided to focus it on something that I know: sociolinguistics and World Englishes. Personally, I see World Englishes as already pretty queer because of its advocating for non-normative views of English variation (B. Kachru 1990; Y. Kachru and Nelson 2006). That is, World Englishes advocates for the acceptance of the notion that the global spread of English has given birth to varieties of English outside of the mainstream ones (i.e. American, Australian, British, and Canadian). Because of this, I use the World Englishes framework to introduce my students to a queered perspective on language ownership, control, and power over who has the right to speak as a legitimate English speaker.

To facilitate this work, we begin reading theoretical and empirical pieces from the field of World Englishes and variationist studies in sociolinguistics early in the course. I encourage my students to keep an open mind about what they will read—especially if they, or their friends, have ever considered them to be an outstanding member of the language police, grammar division. I seek to expose them to a wide swath of the different kinds of Englishes out there; so, we read descriptions of Indian English and China English. But, we also read about how social groups will often recast English in order to take up different identity positionings. It is during this period in the syllabus that we read Heidi Minning's (2004) 'Qwir-English Code-Mixing in Germany: Constructing a Rainbow of Identities.' In this article, Minning discusses how members of the queer community in Germany will utilize their multilingual (German/English) resources in creative ways to build locally relevant identities that will give them access to, and cultural capital in, the German LGBTQ+ community. Central to this is identity work is the act of code mixing, or strategically blending features of two, or more, linguistic systems. I have the students engage with this piece for a couple of reasons. First, it allows them to see that communities of speakers will use language in different ways—some of which may even violate what is considered 'normal' or 'appropriate'. Second, the article highlights for them the fact that these uses of language may be central parts of identity performances that mark a person as either being a member of a particular group or as an outsider. Third, it begins to get them thinking about how sexuality and language go hand-in-hand—especially about how non-normative sexual identities often are required to engage in creative, systematic, non-normative language use to carve out a unique identity position separate from mainstream (read: heterosexual) society.

I also include at least one short novel on the syllabus that was written in either China or Sri Lankan English that explicitly deals with LGBTQ+ issues in the respective country. In the past, I have used books like Ha Jin's (2001) *The Bridegroom* and Shyam Selvadurai's *Funny Boy* (1994). While our primary focus is on how the authors of these texts have used a non-mainstream, non-normative variety of English to construct a text that is better able to speak to Chinese or Sri Lankan concerns respectively, the students gravitate towards discussions of sexuality and how it is perceived and regulated by socially significant others—families, governments, churches, etc. Since I teach sections with over 75% enrolments of L2 English speakers, I encourage them to consider these issues as they may have manifested in their lives, those of their friends and families, and so on in their home contexts. It is also at this point that I begin sharing my own experiences as a gay foreign national living and working outside of my home country and learning to (re)do gay in a second language. At the end of the course, some students choose to engage more deeply with LGBTQ+ issues and being an L2 English user or LGBTQ+ issues in contact literatures. Each semester that I have taught the course, a little over 1/3 of the students have chosen to engage in expanded explorations of these topics in their final papers. Many students find the experience of being in a course with a queered pedagogical approach to be empowering. To quote one student, with whom I have since co-authored a short teaching paper in *TESOL Journal*:

> the most exciting part of the course came as we were engaging with queer contact literatures ... [it] helped me to have a better understanding of the LGBTQ+ community through contact with the topic both in and out of the classroom...[it was not preachy or imposing. Instead, I came to a better understanding of identity in the postmodern world, helping me to be a more respectfully and critically involved student.
>
> (Paiz and Zhu 2018: 3–4)

Graduate Professional Literacy Courses

The goal of many graduate courses is to help students to professionalize into their chosen disciplines (see Casanave and Li 2008; Cho 2013; Hyland 2004). While the primary focus is on helping the student to enculturate in a way that grants them recognition by their disciplinary peers, this does not mean that there is no room to queer graduate education in all disciplines (see, for example, Maritz and Prinsloo 2015). The challenge at the graduate level is to find disciplinarily situated ways in which to make queer-informed pedagogies relevant to the work that the student is completing. Elsewhere, I have regularly argued for the need to queer graduate education for future TESOL practitioners, something which has fed into the work in this book (Paiz 2018; Paiz and Zhu 2018). Queering graduate education, I have argued, must involve making space in the curriculum for readings from the field's LGBTQ+ and queer aligned interest sections. Moreover, and echoing Maritz and Prinsloo (2015), it cannot be left up to the students. So, what does this look like in practice in disciplines outside of TESOL/ALx?

Starting in 2016, I was granted a courtesy appointment with New York University's Silver School of Social Work to teach a graduate literacy course for their L2 English students. I would begin each iteration of the course by positioning myself as an active scholar and an experienced L2 literacy teacher—sharing my teaching experiences as well as my research and scholarly agenda. I would share with them why I was motivated to investigate issues of LGBTQ+ inclusion in the field of English language teaching and learning before inviting them to reflect on how they understand the field of social work and what they see as the major questions and goals of the field. I would then ask them what drew them to the field. Each semester, at least one of my students identified working with LGBTQ+ elderly or youth as one of their core motivations for entering the field of social work. I find that this act, of asking students to identify what they see as the breadths of their field and their core interests, is useful in showing them just how dappled and variegated a discipline truly is—often stretching beyond what we see as its conventional borders.

As we move through the semester, I would make it a point of including readings and example texts that covered a range of topics. So, when we worked on writing policy briefings, I would include one focused on elder care and one focused on trans youth in schools. We would use these texts not only as exemplars of the genre but also to begin interrogating how the clinical social worker can move beyond potentially reductive, othering views of marginalized people in order to advocate on their behalf and to, where necessary, speak truth to power (see Green and Simon 2012). It was here, as we started discussing advocacy and pushing back against discriminatory policies (speaking truth to power), that we were able to start asking the critical, problematizing questions that, to me, help to define queer inquiry—What is the status quo? Who benefits from its maintenance? How can it be challenged to improve the lived conditions of those in power-under positions in society? I would then encourage students to seek out how they could apply these questions to their areas of interest, which we shared in online reflection blogs throughout the semester.

While it has been easy for me to think of ways to queer the classroom in the so-called soft and human sciences classrooms, it has been harder to consider what this might look like in classes founded on the hard sciences and their application. For example, I now teach in an applied English studies programme at a private, research-intensive university in Washington, DC. Many of the students come from our School of Engineering and Applied Sciences, which has forced me to think of how queer inquiry-based pedagogy can be applied in a way that is accessible and meaningful to these students. Here, turning to insights from Leyva, Massa, and Battey (2016) in the field of engineering education has been helpful. They point to the fact that many of the probing and problematizing questions favoured in queer inquiry can be applied to questions of engineering and design. Here, however, the focus may be shifted away from matters of sexuality and sexual identity and moved towards a focus on culture, gender, able-bodiedness. The goal in queer engineering education is the same as in any other queered classroom space, which is to get students thinking critically about how 'doing it the way it has always been done' can shut certain groups out of mainstream conversations. Thinking specifically about engineering disciplines may also require students to take more ownership over issues of usability and accessibility (see Krug 2009).

Community ESL Tutorials

Community ESL programmes often provide low cost or free ESL courses to adult learners in the local region (see Morgan 2002; Skilton-Silverster 2002). These courses often serve immigrant and migrant adults that come from a variety of socioeconomic and linguistic backgrounds. Moreover, the student-attendees often bring with them a range of exposures to formalized English language learning and proficiency levels. Additionally, community ESL programmes are offered by many types of institutions—from religious to education to local governments—and can be taught by individuals with a wide range of teaching experiences. Typically, they are taught by volunteers who may have little or no formal training in TESOL, or they may be offered by universities as part of their engagement activities and are taught by novice teachers.

For example, the Basic ESL Tutorial that was hosted by the English Department at the University of Toledo was free to individuals living throughout the greater Toledo area and was taught by graduate students in the MA TESL programme (University of Toledo 2017). The Basic ESL Tutorial was slated as providing students with introductory lessons in daily-use English, but the students enrolled often range from true beginner to low intermediate in proficiency. And, while the focus is on survival English, there is still the possibility to queer the classroom practice to the benefit of the students that enrol in the course. For example, lessons that are centred around the family tree can be altered to focus on non-nuclear family structures—showcasing family patterns that have same-sex parents, single parents, etc. Additionally, lessons on gender and health can provide students with a critically informed view of gender by including mention of non-binary pronouns. Moreover, lessons on health and the body can take a queered perspective by including visible and non-judgmental representations of disabled bodies. In all of these cases, judgment-free representation is the key for the educator, highlighting these non-normative lives and bodies in ways that model respectful engagement for the lower-proficiency students.

Unlike in the other class types discussed above, the goal in the community-based ESL programme may not be an explicit engagement with, and hopeful adoption of, guiding critical questions. Instead, the educator will be working to trouble normative views of language, the host society, and the body through careful lesson planning and modelling respectful engagement and representation in lessons and instructional materials. This does not mean, however, that if normative classroom discourses occur or disrespectful behaviours do manifest that they should not be challenged. They most certainly should. But, in the community ESL programme, especially at the lower-proficiency levels, the end goal becomes awareness raising and not necessarily the inculcation of a critical attitude. While this may seem to be a conservative approach to queering the community ESL classroom, I believe that it is still in line with Brian Morgan's (2002) recommendations to allow critical ALx to inform our teaching in these programmes and to influence our pedagogical practices. Deeper critical engagement, like that discussed in the previous three sub-sections, above, can come after the linguistic foundation and early acculturation to the local context has been achieved.

Now that I have provided examples of queering different kinds of university and adult learning contexts, I will discuss how you can build your own queer toolkit. It is important to think of this as a tool kit, as opposed to a single pedagogical approach because the *how* of queering the classroom is largely context depending and requires considering your goals as an educator, the outcomes outlined by the curriculum, your local and institutional culture, as well as the various classroom stakeholders. That is, no single queer pedagogical approach will be universally appropriate. Moreover, many queer theorists and educators would argue that to advocate for a single queer pedagogy would, in and of itself, be rather unqueer (see Alexander 2008; Britzman 1995; Waite 2017).

Building Your Queer Inquiry Pedagogical Toolkit

> Ultimately, queer pedagogy entails decentering dominant cultural assumptions, exploring the facets of the geography of normalization, and interrogating the self and the implications of affiliation.
>
> —Amy Winans (2006: 106)

> Teaching queer means risking failure; it means opening conversations that cannot be closed.
>
> —Jacqueline Rhodes (2015)

As we move through exploring how to build your queer pedagogical toolkit, I want you to keep the above quotes in mind. In one way or another, they are central to what we do when we attempt to queer the English language classroom. I would add, that getting students comfortable with this kind of critical work and with doing it using the gamut of their linguistics resources is also an important consideration. This section will be the springboard for later chapters in this book. Here, I will be introducing you to the tools in your queer toolkit and connecting them back to the discussion so far, but I will be exploring them in finer detail in later chapters. This section is organized so that if there is a section that catches your interest, you will be able to skip to the chapter that discusses it further so that you can take agency over your engagement with this material in ways that are relevant to your current professional development needs.

There are, broadly speaking, two central tools in your toolkit. The primary one is the queer inquiry framework (Nelson 2006, 2009). This framework provides us with guiding questions and attitudes to queer our practice in ways that will address issues of classroom equity for sexual minorities. It is based on the notion of continually questioning and attempting to lay bare the normative social discourses around us and in which our students and we are situated relative to each other and society by said discourses.

Said another way, the primary and most potent tool in your queer toolkit is to ask questions like:

- Why is * so?[3]
- What conditions have led to * being view/valued/talked about in the way that it has?
- Who benefits from * being held in a position of power over another group, or one group being held in power under a dominant one?
- What needs to change for * to move from a marginalized, peripheral position to a more accepted central one?
- What attitudes and biases and am I bringing with me that I will need to control for to provide my students with an even and fair educational experience?

Using these questions as you plan lessons, and helping students become comfortable with asking them, is an important part of the queer inquiry-based pedagogy that I am advocating for here.

The second major tool that you have in your toolkit is what Pennycook (2001) identified as a restive problematizing of what we assume to know and to be true. I would argue that, as educators seeking to queer our practice, we must go one step further to utilize a *dialogic, contextually responsive problematizing*. That is, we cannot just import our notions of sexuality and sexual identity to new national or educational context without first attempting to put our thoughts and beliefs about sexual diversity and equity into dialogue with locally relevant ways of being, knowing, and expressing queerness. For example, the lived experiences and social orientations of women who have sex with women in Egypt is not the same as a lesbian woman in urban Canada (see Khayatt 2003). Therefore, we must guard against essentializing, reductivist views of queer lives and queer bodies as we attempt to make our classrooms more inclusive, which can lead to a challenge with managing just how much to unpack for students in your language classes.[4] In this regards, dialogic, contextually responsive problematizing is often greatly aided by working in tandem with students and local community contacts to better understand local LGBTQ+ lives and experiences. Next, I am going to introduce you to three other parts of a queer toolkit.

Challenging Classrooms and Materials

Later in this book, I am going to discuss the need to reflect on and to challenge classroom practices, discourses, and materials that help to reinforce and recreate normative discourses about sexual identity and language learning. When looking at normative classroom practices, this can mean calling on ourselves to reflect critically on how we use the classroom space to, even tacitly, bolster these norms through how we design the space, how we conduct ourselves as a teacher, or even the pre-class time small talk that we make. For example, in decorating the language classroom in the K-12 context, do the visual materials show a variety of peoples and bodies engaged in language learning? Or, does the motivational poster only feature able-bodied, stereotypically gendered and attired individuals? In the university classroom, do the pre-class questions that focus on out of class life, presume that students are either (a) heterosexual or (b) financially secure and able to engage in the leisure life of the university (see, for example, Fraiberg, Wang, and You 2017; Vandrick 1997)?

Elsewhere, I have argued that ESL texts and textbooks are dominantly heteronormative in the worldview that they present to our students; moreover, this ideological bent can unduly influence the work of early service educators (Paiz 2015a, 2018). We see this heteronormativity reflected to us and our students in the narratives about the target society that the texts choose to include, as well as in the images about language learners and native speakers that they choose to include. This means that we must constantly be seeking ways to queer these materials, as well as our practices. Therefore, an essential part of your toolkit will be a sensitivity to how dominant, normative discourse may be permeating your classroom, your interaction with students, and how the materials that are provided to the students may unwittingly reinforce the notion that LGBTQ+ lives are either invisible or not of consequence. This can lead to LGBTQ+ students being silenced in the classroom, contributing to negative social and educational outcomes.

Managing Reactions and Challenges

Managing the reactions of students, parents, and administrators will be a crucial part of your queer toolkit. In my personal efforts, I have run into colleagues who feel that using queer pedagogies is either (a) unethical because it imparts an ideological bias on my teaching or (b) is unjust because it unnecessarily favours LGBTQ+ students. It is not uncommon to run into such reactions from the various stakeholders in our classrooms. I find that the growing body of LGBTQ+ research in TESOL and ALx, as well as the increasing focus on diversity, equity, and inclusion at Western universities, is a good guide to help in managing these reactions. In Chapter 5, I will take a more in-depth look at some tools—like anonymized *Google Forms* responses—that you can use to gain feedback from students. Additionally, I will provide some personal insights on handling difficult conversations about queering the classroom with parents and administrators.

Setting Goals and Outcomes

Identifying and clearly articulating goals for your efforts to queer the classroom, as well as likely educational/developmental outcomes for your students, is another important tool to deploy in your efforts to create more inclusive spaces. Recently, Krause (2017) identified the need to set realistic goals for queering educational practice to prevent teacher disillusionment. By modifying Bennett's (2013) paradigm of intercultural communication, Krause (2017) underscored the importance of setting realistic goals for queering practice that were targeted not at radical changes in students' worldviews or beliefs, but on moving the needle from disengagement/discomfort to fuller, respectful engagement with queer issues and lives. In Chapter 6, we will look more closely at this tool as we round out your queer toolkit.

Conclusion

I want to end this chapter with a certain contradiction, a possible paradox. Throughout this chapter, I have shared my queer inquiry-based approach to teaching with you through the provided examples. I have also suggested, in a seemingly uncomplicated, hierarchical manner, several useful tools to have in your own toolkit. This presentation gives the illusion that queering the classroom, at least as I am advocating for it, is linear, is straightforward, without seeming self-contradiction or fatal paradoxes. Many queer theorists and scholars would disagree with this style of presentation. Stacey Waite, in her book *Teaching Queer: Radical Possibilities for Writing and*

Knowing ends her chapter on pedagogy by saying, 'To make a list would be to make linear what is not linear; it would suggest as whole what is already incomplete; it would be to formulate notions that slip through [our] fingers as they take form' (Waite 2017: 124). And, theorists like Butler, Jagose, and Sullivan would all likely agree that if we outline a rigid form for queer pedagogy—if we say it (can) look(s) like this, or it can do these things—we are necessarily engaging in a normative, and therefore not very queer, act.

However, this is where I must disagree with them. If we fail to, at least temporarily, make queer theory and queer pedagogy knowable, how can we engage with it? How can we make it useful to practitioners in their classrooms? How can it come to *mean* anything useful and potentially transformative to our students? I do not believe it can. I believe we must, as I have sought here and throughout this book, at least temporarily pin down queer pedagogy so that we can have a shared frame of reference to begin our work of queering our practice and our classes. Once this is done, we go back, we requeer it. Even Butler (1990) concedes that we must have norms and that temporary crystallization is important because it is part of a cycle of renewal and requeering. If anything, see what is in this book as a starting point. Find ways it fits in to your practice and your context. Then, find ways to return to it, to requeer it. In short, find ways to get comfortable with knowing, unknowing, and reknowing what it means to make your classes more inclusive, more equitable and engaged spaces.

Key Takeaways

For this chapter, the crucial points revolve around the issues that queering the classroom seeks to lay bare for educator and student alike, the philosophical starting points of queer inquiry-based pedagogy, and a description of this pedagogical approach and the tools that it makes available to the practitioners as they engage in the work of queering their practice. So, distilling the important points into some takeaways for you, they would be the following:

- Queering the classroom seeks to lay bare important social issues for students that include: the regulation of sexuality and sexuality identity; the need for critical engagement with the idea that normative discourses unduly advantage some while disadvantaging others; the need to critically reflect on how we use language to reinforce normative worldviews; and, the need to push beyond our comfort zones to engage more fully with social justice considerations.

- The philosophical starting points of many queer inquiry-based pedagogies begin from considering how we co-construct knowledge with the others with whom we interact daily before moving on to consider how we must challenge discourses that normalize certain ways of life over others in a zero-sum fashion in the hopes of fostering increased ownership over learning and engagement in our students.
- There is no single way to queer the classroom. This book shows you one of the ways and equips you with tools to queer your own practice.

Reflexive Practice Prompt

To help stimulate your reflection on the topics discussed in this chapter, you can make use of the following questions:

- What is the state of institutional environment towards social justice issues (e.g. race, gender, sexuality, class, etc.) and how might it facilitate or hinder my efforts?
- What institutional/programmatic/disciplinary peers can I turn to for help as I attempt to queer my pedagogy?
- What goals do I have for myself as I begin to work towards building more LGBTQ+ educational spaces and interventions?

3

Troubling Normative Classroom Spaces

AT A GLANCE

Introduction

With the theoretical and conceptual frameworks established, it is now time to turn our focus to the actual work of queering classroom practice in English language classrooms. This chapter provides you with actionable guidance for troubling normative classrooms spaces so that you can work to make them more critically aware and inclusive spaces. Troubling normative classes and educational practices requires the educator to be, as described by Alistair Pennycook (2001), engaged in a restive problematizing of what has seemingly always been assumed true, valid, and valued. Being a restive problematizer means laying bare and interrogating assumptions about how the world around us works. In the context of the language classroom, it requires us to ask whether or not our practices, materials, and spaces are not only accessible to all but are inclusive of all. Now, that may sound as if this chapter will advocate for taking a 'kitchen sink' approach to queering the classroom, but it most certainly will not. Queering the classroom, troubling normativity in all its forms, never means being inclusive to the point that our lessons get stuck in a morass of covering every single iteration of identity that there is. Take teaching the family as an example. Queering our teaching does not mean that our materials must include every single family configuration known to humankind—a daunting task that would have us spending at least two months teaching the family and the different ways of referring to it in English speaking contexts. Instead, building an inclusive classroom means applying the attitudes mentioned in previous chapters to ensure that there is *space* for lives and bodies that deviate from the mainstream—transgressive lives and bodies that buck the norm and that may, therefore, be in a position of power under and of marginalization.

This approach to teaching matters because, as mentioned in previous chapters, there is a lot at stake when we allow normative practices and classrooms to go unchecked. Failing to build inclusive pedagogies and classrooms can silence student voices, removing their perspectives and contributions from the class. Moreover, normative classroom environments coupled with deficit views of language learners can mean that when students do attempt to make authentic contributions that they positioned as if they are as missing the point of the lesson (see Liddicoat 2009). Additionally, allowing normative classrooms and educational practices to go uncheck serves to replicate an inequitable status quo; one that maintains power and privilege for the mainstream (read: white, able-bodied, monogamous, heterosexual community), while marginalizing all who deviate from the norm. As Vandrick (1997, 2001) has shown, this can have disastrous effects on learners as it threatens their core sense of self and may lead them to mitigate that threat by hiding or masking that identity—diverting valuable cognitive and affective energies away from language learning. Finally, normative classes and pedagogies can effectively shut down language learning and second language acquisition by making the classroom seem unwelcoming to LGBTQ+ and ally students and sapping them of their motivation to learn when their meaningful and honest contributions are met with awkward silences, heteronormative recasts, or ignored altogether (see Dörneyi and Uchida 2009 for a discussion on motivation and self in L2 learning/acquisition).

Before continuing, however, I want to offer a quick word on the notion of taking a neutral tact. It can be tempting to take this approach, to not trouble normative educational practice out of concerns about appearances, student reactions, or disrupting the status quo. The classroom has carried on in its seemingly 'natural' state for quite some time, and most people have no issues with it. If a student does wonder why there is a lack of representation and inclusion of diverse voices and lives, then they can find ways to inject them into the classroom on their own—because that is how we foster student agency and interest in the teaching/learning endeavour. I fear that I must point out that there is no such thing as neutrality when it comes to issues of diversity, equity, inclusion, and engagement. As I and others have argued elsewhere, the decision *not* to do something—in this case not to queer the classroom—is itself an ideological act because teaching is always already ideologically fraught (Paiz 2018; Waite 2017). So, to not attempt to make the classroom more inclusive of sexual and gender minorities is not a values-neutral, ideologically impartial act. Being 'neutral' is just as values-laden and ideologically bent as taking action to either make educational practices more inclusive or more normative.[1]

Therefore, this chapter will offer guidance to practitioners as they seek to trouble normative classes and to build more inclusive educational practices. It will do this by offering practical advice on identifying normative classrooms by considering their physical characteristics and the teaching methods/materials used in them. A crucial part of this conversation will focus on looking at the underlying forces that encourage normative spaces in education, which includes societal and institutional forces, as well as individual teaching philosophies, among other concerns. Throughout the first half of this chapter, I will also discuss some of the potential threats that these concerns may pose to language learning and acquisition. In the second half of this chapter, I will provide you advice for how to trouble normative classrooms by zeroing in on teacher education/mentoring, curricular issues, and classroom practices. This discussion will make use of example lessons and activities that can then serve as a foundation for your efforts to queer your teaching and to create more inclusive classroom spaces.

Describing Normative Classrooms

Recall from earlier chapters that heteronormativity is the portrayal of reproductive, monogamous heterosexuality as the only natural, valid, and valued sexual identity (see Duggan 2002; Nelson 2009; Paiz 2019). In this chapter, we will carry this definition forward while also expanding it to look at normative classroom practices more generally, because queering the classroom goes beyond issues of gender, sex, and sexuality to touch on resisting all forms of normativity. So, what do normative classrooms look like? How do we know one when we see one? Alternatively, a better question would be how can I spot a normative class *in situ*, as the classroom's spaces and its normativeness or criticality/transgressiveness tend to be emergent. That is, an otherwise normative class may have moments that push against normativity in a particular form, but overall remain a site of enforcing educational and societal norms. This means, of course, that the forms that normative classroom spaces can take are myriad and can be linked variously to issues ranging from the physical classroom space to the actual teaching practices being deployed therein.

The space that our classrooms occupy—whether physical or digital—can have profound impacts on students, educators, and the teaching/learning process. Because of the importance of space, it has received increased attention in recent years, with scholars investigating everything from physical layout, to colour, decoration, access to natural light and fresh air, and web-based usability and accessibility in and across cultures and age groups (see Barrett, Zhang, Moffat, and Kobbacy 2013; Blythe, 2001; Gaines and Curry 2011; Gherwash and Paiz n.d.). It can be tempting when thinking about normative classrooms to think of the traditional teacher-centred layout, as has been described in works such as Dick (1997) or Weinstein (1981), where there is a desk or technology podium at the front of the room, along with some combination of projector screen, TV monitor, and/or dry erase/chalkboard and rows of tables and chairs or desks for the students. This teacher-centred architecture has been heavily critiqued as not being a productive learning environment (Barrett, Davies, Zhang, and Barrett 2015) and not conducive to facilitating student agency (Blewett, Morris, and Rule 2016). However, even more student-centred, de-centralized layouts, such as organizing the room in a circular format have been critiqued for not addressing the core issue of facilitating student-centred learning (e.g. Housego and Burns 1994).

It is, perhaps, possible to read these spaces as variously normative depending on the setting. For example, the traditional teacher-centred classroom layout is indeed normative in that it can help maintain the traditional power structures of the teacher or professor as the end-point of knowledge and authority in the classroom. Meanwhile, the so-called student-centred classroom, with its circles and open spaces can be just as normative when it is the go-to classroom configuration in an institution—it delimits for students acceptable identities, marking non-conforming students as outside of the norm and therefore deficient in some way. Here, I would echo Blewett, Morris, and Rule (2016) and Barrett, Davies, Zhang, and Barrett (2015) in saying that what matters much more is how the teacher *makes use of that space* to create an inviting classroom setting that troubles normative discourses of teacher/student and their relationship and that facilitates increasing student agency over their learning. For example, moving around the classroom and not getting anchored to the technology podium/lectern, or moving out of the typical classroom configurations when possible to a more open concept space for activities like station teaching can be much more effective at troubling normative spaces (see Scruggs, Masteropieri, and McDuffie 2007). Beyond physical layout, the décor of a classroom can also reinforce normative discourses about student identities—from ableist to gender normative to heteronormative ones. For example, something seemingly as innocuous as coloured name badges for a behaviour board can become problematic if only traditionally masculine colours (e.g. blues, reds, tans, etc.) are used for the male-presenting students and feminine colours (e.g. pinks, violets, pastel shades, etc.) for the female-presenting students. Likewise, classroom posters can also reinforce normative discourses, contributing to a normative classroom environment. For example, Kaplan Early Learning produces a well-rated 'Families of the World Poster Set' for display in classrooms. The set of eight posters feature families of various ethnicities and sizes. While this poster set could indeed be lauded for its ethnic diversity, a quick glance shows that all of these images show only heterosexual, homoracial nuclear families. Both of these examples showcase the potentials ways that normative discourses, specifically heteronormative ones, in this case, can creep into the classroom through seemingly innocuous design and decorating decisions. Moreover, they are decisions that may not rise to the level of conscious awareness for the educator as ones that could potentially contribute to a normative classroom space when considered in the larger context of the sheer amount of planning that goes into preparing for a new academic year. However, once we are aware of the potential

Figure 3.1 Screenshot of Trend Enterprises bulletin board sets showing a student that uses a wheelchair (left) and a female firefighter (right).

Retrieved from https://michaels.com

issues of normative classroom spaces we can begin to seek out alternative resources that begin to trouble normative discourses about race, ableism, gender, and sexuality. For example, Figure 3.1 shows some great examples of inclusive classroom design elements that begin to trouble normative discourses (ableism and gender).

More often, however, normative classroom spaces are more easily identified by the curricular decisions and teaching practices of the educator. Recall, for example, the vignette from Chapter 1 that discussed how the student in the Spanish as a foreign language classroom was cast as a deficient language learner when they (a cisgender male) performed a homosexual identity in response to the teacher's question about their girlfriend. Elsewhere, I provide a more detailed analysis of this example (Paiz 2020a). Moreover, it is not only the teacher's repeated attempts to elicit the 'correct' gendered responses from the student that contributes to the heteronormative classroom environment, it is also their reaction when the student more forcefully responds to the attempted correction by unequivocally stating that he is homosexual and referring to his same-sex romantic partner. Specifically, the dialogue recorded by Liddicoat (2009) shows the teacher pause for some time (approximately 0.7 seconds) before moving on to the next student. In other cases, educators may construct more heteronormative educational spaces in a much more combustive

Interaction 2, Class 2—On-Task:
"Can I Discuss any Kind of Prejudice,// Homosexuality?"

T: Number 3 / Report on a situation in which someone/ in which someone/ has acted/ has acted/ in a biased way./ Repeating./ Report on a situation/in which someone has- has acted in a biased way.//
Juca: Teacher, / in question 3/ can I discuss any kind of prejudice,// homosexuality?//
T: ( )Listen,/ I want you to give a report in a respectful manner./ If we are going to be disrespectful,/ what was the purpose of last Monday's reading of the text,/ today's discussion,/ and what is the purpose of the discussion we are having now?// If we are going to be disrespectful,/ I am going to put my books away/ and go home./ we are wasting time here.//
Rico: You're such a brat/ Why are you talking about this now?
Tiago: Teacher, go a bit slower!//
Ps: ( )
T: Question 4, shhh.//
Tiago: Slow down, teacher!/ Slow down.//
Ps: ( )
Tiago: Slow down, please!//
T: ( )
Tiago: I am behind.//
T: I hope you make a respectful report.//
Rico: Great!/ Great!//
T: What was the purpose of today's discussion?//

Figure 3.2 Brazilian Portuguese heritage language classroom assignment negotiation interaction.

Source: Moita-Lopes (2006: 37–38)

manner. For example, looking closer at an excerpt from Moita-Lopes (2006) shows one teacher's rather reactionary outburst when a student asks if they can write their paper on the discrimination faced by the homosexual community in Brazil (Figure 3.2; for analysis see Paiz 2020a). Before we can go about the work of troubling and transforming normative classroom spaces, it may be helpful to understand better some of the forces at work that may motivate and maintain heteronormative discourses.

Contributing Forces that Drive Normativity in the Language Classroom

There are a range of influencers that contribute to the maintenance and replication of normative discourses in English language classrooms—ranging from the societal to the institutional to the personal. Working from the top-down, societal concerns are a prime driver of normative approaches to ELT. National orientations towards diversity-related topics can motivate educators to either engage or disengage with specific topics, as well as inform their approach to doing so. For example, the increased focus on gender disparity in the United States has driven not only language change—with sometimes mixed reactions—[2] but also curricular innovations. In the case of LGBTQ+ considerations, even more progressive national contexts can take a conservative bent when it comes to the inclusion of LGBTQ+ material into formalized educational settings. Alexander (2008) maintains that sexuality has become a crucial part of US, and perhaps Western, discourses, a fact that is attested to with a review of cultural artefacts. There has been a considerable increase in LGBTQ+ representation in popular media—from comic books (Marvel's Iceman and DC's Batwoman) to television shows (Netflix's *Queer Eye for the Straight Guy* or CBS' *Star Trek Discovery*). Additionally, LGBTQ+ penetration into both traditional and social media has seen a marked uptick in the past 15 years.[3] Despite this, there is still a great deal of pushback in many Western contexts when LGBTQ+ issues are made a part of the classroom (see Quinlan 2016 for the US context, and Ullman and Ferfolja 2016 for the Australian context). Taken together, these contribute to societal contexts where there are polyvocal calls both for more and no LGBTQ+-inclusion in classrooms, leaving many teachers to take a more conservative approach in their teaching. Often, this manifests as non-engagement with LGBTQ+ issues. Or, as in the example above (see Figure 3.2), to actively shut down LGBTQ+-focused conversations.

Institutionally speaking, there may be either an institutional culture or explicit mandate, to steer clear of politically charged, potentially sensitive topics, of which LGBTQ+ concerns are often classed. This stance can, of course, contribute to the emergence and maintenance of normative classroom environments. Institutionally backed normativity may emerge either implicitly through negative administrative feedback when teachers broach the idea of building LGBTQ+ lessons or of engaging with the notion of inclusive sexual literacy. Alternatively, it may come about through explicit policy decisions at the institutional level, as exists at many religious institutions. For example, the doctrinal and mission statements of Liberty University in Lynchburg, Virginia aligns very clearly with broader Evangelical beliefs, including a hostile view towards LGBTQ+

lives (compare Board of Trustees 2014 and Liberty University 2019 versus Assemblies of God 2019). Institutional standings like this directly contribute to normative, if not downright homo- and transphobic classrooms because they squelch a teacher's willingness to consider transformative, emancipatory pedagogies. It happens by, either purposefully or incidentally, creating an environment of fear—one where the educator, fearing either reprisals or dismissal, has no choice but to let marginalizing, heteronormative discourses to persist even when they are counter to their personal beliefs.

Finally, individual teaching philosophies can contribute to the maintenance of normative classroom spaces. Whether it is grounded in an allegedly apolitical ideology or a socially conservative one that takes exception to LGBTQ+ issues, an individual's teaching philosophy can drive them to work towards minimizing or excluding queer voices and perspectives in the classroom. Returning to the example of my NYU Shanghai colleague from chapter one, this is an individual who would likely work towards minimizing LGBTQ+ content in their classes because they viewed the EL classroom as one where the only focus should be on the more concrete aspects of language—lexis, syntax, pronunciation, etc. Despite their personal connections to the LGBTQ+ community, their teaching philosophy was one that rather blatantly worked to maintain heteronormative discourses in their classroom—a move which, in my opinion, creates certain risks for all students.

What Is at Stake in Normative Classrooms

Before moving on, I want to use this section to gather the threads about this topic that have been initially presented throughout the first two chapters. I want to lay out, however briefly, a clear and concise statement of what is in jeopardy in classrooms where heteronormative discourses are left unchallenged either because we think 'political' topics have no place in ELT, we're uncomfortable with LGBTQ+ issues, or we just don't know how to handle them in a way that we feel would be pedagogically ethical in our local context. At the very least, we risk making LGBTQ+-identified students feel as if they are marginal in our classroom spaces. Recent research looking at factors that make women feel out of place in STEM undergraduate programmes provides an example of what happens when students are rendered invisible. Cheryan, Plaut, Handron, and Hudson (2013), for example, have shown that the fact that these students, especially women of colour, feel marginalized by a lack of representation—in the professoriate, in professional panels, in the literature, in the makeup of the classroom—has contributed to decreased initial interest in STEM majors; moreover, this lack of representation also plays a marked role in attrition from these programmes. Similar studies have not been carried out in the English language classroom, perhaps because of the material drive to acquire English for many that see it as a ticket to social or professional advancement (see Kachru 2006). However, the work of Ashely Moore (2013, 2016) does show, that some students view the language classroom and acquiring English as a critical step in gaining access to global LGBTQ+ communities and to liberating a facet of their social identity that may be highly stigmatized in their local context. Moore's work starkly underscores how the heteronormative language classroom can also play a central role in replicating marginalizing discourses.

Recent research from GLSEN (2017), a K-12 educational research and advocacy group in the United States shows that LGBTQ+ youth in American schools feel under-represented in the curriculum; and, even if their teachers are supportive, this invisibility can create issues with coming forward about bullying or abuse. Moreover, GLSEN (2017) research shows that LGBTQ+ youth are still at risk in classroom settings, especially transgender and gender non-conforming students who report exceptionally high rates of verbal and physical abuse. All of this points rather starkly to the fact that normative educational spaces not only make it so that students cannot imagine themselves as part of the classroom, it also contributes to the replication of broader social issues that can put student safety at risk. This jeopardy is, I believe, amplified for students who are acquiring English as an additional language, as English may be their primary vehicle of expressing concerns over their health and well-being to authority figures (e.g. teachers, principals, social workers, etc.) that could intervene to help ensure their safety.

Taken together, this makes resoundingly clear what is at risk in a normative classroom environment—the continued silencing of marginalized individuals and the perpetuation of social discourses that can contribute to psychological and physical harm. Therefore, active steps must be taken to create inclusive classroom and institutional settings that push back against marginalizing, normative discourses. The pedagogy advocated for in this chapter is one example, but it only addresses pedagogical and curricular issues, broader institutional issues must be still be addressed, as I have argued elsewhere (see Paiz 2019, 2020a).

Troubling Normative Practices

Remediating normative classroom practices begins with adjusting our pedagogical approach. While a general sketch of a queer pedagogy was presented in Chapter 2, this section is going to focus on concrete examples of classroom practices and activities that you can deploy in your teaching. I will begin this section with some general recommendations for everyday interactions before moving on to some specific activities that may be adapted to your specific classroom needs. These are activities that have been used to varying degrees in my teaching, my work as a teacher education consultant, or that I have modified from existing literature on queering classroom practice for mainstream (read: monolingual, native speaker) classrooms.

Even the simplest of modifications can begin to break down normative classroom practices. In many EL classrooms, we are faced with class sizes that would make our peers in the STEM fields green with envy, with many L2 writing, English for academic purposes (EAP), and intensive English programme (IEP) courses at North American universities capped at between 12 and 25.[4] And, we see similar smaller class sizes as a key selling point of many for-profit EFL programmes worldwide. This smaller class size is not only heralded as critical for supporting language learning/acquisition; it also allows us to form more intimate bonds with our students (see Xu 2001). This state often means that we get to know our students quite well; and, they get to know us. We get comfortable with each other, and the door appears to open to more personal questions as we move through our time together. I cannot count how many times I have been asked if I was married when I was a younger teacher. Now, the assumption is that I *must* be married. So, I often get questions about my wife—or for students that are paying attention, about my spouse. I say all of this to underscore the fact that we engage with our students on a personal level in many EL classrooms. Moreover, many of the mass-produced textbooks that we use encourage this level of engagement by including chapters on family, dating, and relationships and a cross-cultural, as opposed to inter- or transcultural (see Atkinson 2016), view of it.

Make LGBTQ+ Language a Normal Part of the Classroom Discourse

One small change that we can make a more inclusive practice is to make LGBTQ+ language a normal part of classroom discourse. So whenever we discuss dating with our students, instead of using terms like 'girlfriend' when speaking to male-presenting students, or 'boyfriend' when speaking to female-presenting students, using purposefully clunky terminology like 'boyfriend and/or girlfriend' can be more inclusive and open the door to powerful conversations of how we conceive of romantic relations and how they are constructed and constrained through language. I know that this language sounds clunky, and that is on purpose. In my teaching, I will often say things like, 'I get it! College life is tough; remember that Dr Paiz has been there. You're away from home. You're exploring your future profession, some of you may even be looking for boyfriends and/or girlfriends for the first time.' This often comes up during the opening days of the semester as we are discussing strategies for succeeding at an American university. The first couple of times I use this language, I will see students making puzzled faces. And, almost without fail one student will eventually pipe up to ask why I say 'boyfriends and/or girlfriends' when talking to them. It is this act of introducing a seemingly strange and clunky language item that opens the door to conversation. I mention, without making it seem like a problematic or taboo issue, that I say boyfriend and/or girlfriend to acknowledge the fact that I do not know what individual students might be looking for—assuming they even are interested in dating, as many of their American peers might be. So, to be inclusive of everyone—gay, straight, bi, trans, polyamorous, etc.—I use language that I feel is inclusive and allows a student to see themselves reflected in the classroom, because our learning space is an open and inclusive one. After a while, this language and the ideological leaning that it represents gets normalized into classroom discourse, troubling the notion that only straight lives are valid and valued in the classroom space. Eventually, some students pushback on my use of boyfriend and/or girlfriend by asking me, 'What about people that don't want a boyfriend *or* a girlfriend. Like they don't feel like they need one?'

Include LGBTQ+ Language Examples when Discussing Other Aspects of Language

The above question opens the door to another small change that can be made in classroom practice that will allow us to trouble normativity. When students ask the question above, I use a word attack mini-lesson to introduce terms like aromantic and asexual. So, when a student asks, 'What about people that don't want a boyfriend or a girlfriend?' I will respond with, 'Perhaps these people are aromantic asexuals. You're right; the way that I talk doesn't always include people that fall on this part of the spectrum of sexual identity, does it?' I will then write aromantic and asexual on the board, and then ask students if they are familiar with word attack strategies. If they are, I jump into tearing the words apart; if they are not, I will briefly introduce what word attack strategies are used for and then use these two words, plus a few others, to model using word attack strategies. Either way, I will ask my students what words they see in 'aromantic' and 'asexual' that look familiar. Students will often blurt out 'romantic' and 'sexual'. Then, I will ask them what they think the prefix 'a-' might mean in English. After a few rounds of discussion, we will arrive at a meaning for the prefix 'a-', usually meaning something like, 'not' or 'absent' or 'devoid of'. Once we have reached this point, I will then put up a few more words with the 'a-' prefix, such as 'asymptomatic', 'areligious' and 'amoral'. I will then wrap up this part of the mini-lesson by talking about how they can use this strategy when they encounter difficult academic words in their readings for this and other courses.

Another option is to be sure to incorporate LGBTQ+-inclusive language when discussing grammar. For example, in a beginner lesson that focuses on pronouns in English, you might generate a starting list as a class, like the one in Figure 3.3. This co-cognition board was created by asking students 'What words do you know that English uses to talk about other things. For example, when I say, 'They ate lunch together' instead of saying 'Fatima, Junhan, and Santiago ate lunch together'.

Once we have our list, I can then begin breaking it down into plural and singular pronouns by asking additional questions of my students. This is where introducing more inclusive language can come into play. I can then ask the students to work in pairs to sort the list into terms that refer to only one person and terms that can refer to more than one. Afterwards, they put their answers on the board. I will then add, if it is not there

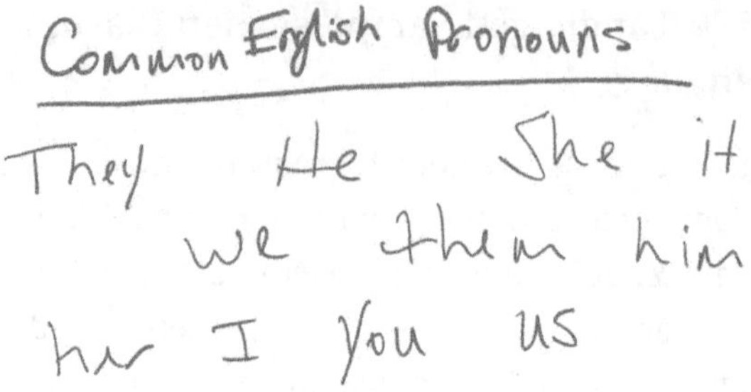

Figure 3.3 First round pronoun co-cognition board from a beginner-level IEP course.

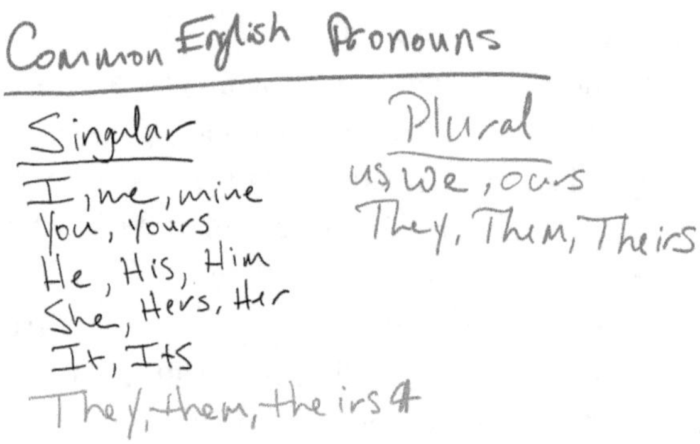

Figure 3.4 Revised pronoun co-cognition board showing inclusive approaches to teaching pronouns.

already 'they, them, their' to the board under the 'Singular' column, as shown in Figure 3.4, above. This often leads to some confusion on the part of the students, which I then clarify that in the United States, 'they, them' and 'their' are acceptable singular, epicene pronouns when you either do not know a person's gender identity or when they use these terms to refer to theirself. While I may not reach 100% clarity on the first pass, this raises students awareness about LGBTQ+-inclusive language while also discussing important grammatical points that are commonly targeted in ESL, EAP, and IEP courses. Moreover, it creates space for continued discussion and clarification around these points. Remember, troubling normative classrooms is not a one and done situation. It is ongoing, emergent, and negotiated.

Make LGBTQ+ Representation a Regular Part of Instruction

Another critical avenue for troubling normative classrooms is to make LGBTQ+ representation a consistent part of instruction. More importantly, this must be done through multimodal means wherever possible. A good example of this is the reading nook or classroom library that may be present in many K-12 settings. Instead of stocking the typical graduated readers, such as the Cambridge English Readers series, which includes stories targeting beginner to advanced proficiency students with plots ranging from comedy, to romance, to action/adventure, you may want to consider finding level appropriate reading materials that include LGBTQ+ characters as their primary focus. Many web-based resources, such as the HRC's Welcoming Schools (2019) site, provide curated lists of grade-appropriate books that feature LGBTQ+ content, such as Richardson and Parnell's (2015) And Tango Makes Three (PreK to 3rd grade), Levy's (2015) The Misadventures of the Family Fletcher (4th to 7th grades), or Podos's (2017) Like Water (8th grade and up). The reason to caution you away from the graduated readers, while they may provide additional important tools for students that are acquiring English an additional/second language, is they have been shown to be predominately heteronormative in their storylines. Moreover, many researchers suggest that this is unlikely to change because of a robust economic imperative for publishers in a global market (see Gray 2013; Paiz 2015a; Smestad 2018).

Another way to make LGBTQ+ issues a regular and sustained part of the classroom is to include LGBTQ+ history and national celebrations in the classroom through time-sensitive décor. Every 11 October is National Coming Out day in the US, and posters and other marketing materials are readily available through organizations like LGBT Network (2019). October in North America and February in the United Kingdom also mark LGBT History Month, which is another opportunity to include LGBTQ+-inclusive feature material in the classroom[5] and to hold special conversations about the evolution of LGBTQ+ rights and attitudes in these national contexts over time. During these discussions, a special focus can be given to individuals like Harvey Milk, Barbara Gittings, Audre Lorde, and Christine Jorgensen—all of whom have advanced LGBTQ+ equality in significant ways.

Additionally, considering more closely the physical classroom space, its layout, and its décor, it is possible to make small changes that begin to trouble more normative environments. For example, if you make use of a behaviour board as part of your classroom management, using gender-neutral colours for students' name cards is one option; alternatively you could allow students to self-select the colours for their nameplates. Or, if your classroom includes posters of important historical figures, including ones that acknowledge the works and sexual identity of LGBTQ+ individuals from around the world is another small change that can go a long way towards creating a more inclusive space.

Make LGBTQ+-inclusive Policies to Drive Classroom Management

It has been reported throughout the literature that a significant concern of teachers when it comes to considering whether or not to queer their practice is how they will respond to homophobia in the classroom (see Coda 2018a; MacDonald 2015; Merse 2017). While these concerns are justifiable, as homophobia can contribute to a toxic classroom environment if left unchecked, worries over opening the door to homophobic responses is not enough to discount the importance of creating inclusive classroom spaces and practices. Indeed, to use this worry as the foundation for *not* actively queering the classroom replicates and maintains heteronormative discourses in our classes. To that end, I believe that having LGBTQ+-inclusive policies in place from day one is critical to assuaging teachers' worries about homophobic outbursts. Additionally, it is important to have explicit course policies in place to provide the practitioner with reliable tools to guide decision making when toxic events do occur. Moreover, transparency with our students helps establish expectations and to facilitate what is expected of them in the course beyond time, attention, and academic ability.

Any classroom policy should be modelled around the idea of *respectful engagement*. I often outline respectful engagement to my students like this, 'we don't have to agree on anything; you don't have to believe what I, or others, believe; nor do you have to value what I, or others value. But, you must be able to calmly, thoughtfully, and respectfully voice any disagreement that you have'. That is, you must be here and at least listen. You do not have to change your whole worldview, but you must be a full part of the educational endeavours of our shared learning space.

Moreover, any classroom policy must also include explanations for what will happen if passions—either pro- or anti-gay—get inflamed. While some passionate debate can be good and provide a teachable moment for how to use language to disagree in English respectfully, there are some moments that get so heated that their potential toxicity far outweighs their educational value. I tell my students that in these cases, I will use my judgement and feedback from the class, and may decide that we need to hit the pause button for the day. We are not going to end the conversation; we're just going to put a pin in it until all parties can calm down and reflect on the conversation, their beliefs, and their attitudes in a more critical manner. I may then provide a date when we will resume the conversation and some guiding questions to think about in the meantime.

Another inclusive policy to help facilitate respectful engagement is focused on interpersonal interactions in class. Having a policy that requires students and teachers alike to use each other's preferred names and pronouns can go a long way towards creating an inclusive classroom space modelled on respectful engagement. This is important because birth names, which may be legally required to appear on classroom rosters in some jurisdictions, can be a source of anxiety for transgender individuals because of the emotions connected to it (e.g. Grossman and D'augelli 2006; Ingnatavicius 2013). There are several ways to facilitate the use of preferred names and pronouns in the classroom. Perhaps the most explicit way is to have every member of the class, the teacher included, make a name tent or wear a name badge with their preferred name and to affix a preferred pronoun sticker to the name tent (see Figure 3.5 for examples of pronoun stickers).[6] For a more subtle approach, and one that should be deployed along a more explicit lesson on pronouns later on (see above), the teacher can always circulate a seating chart or sign-in sheet where students provide their preferred names and tick off a box next to their preferred pronouns—this can also be distributed digitally through a platform like Google Forms or Qualtrix to provide added confidentiality. An important note here is that under no circumstances should the educator out transgender students as trans by providing their birth names or drawing attention to their transgender status. Doing so would break down the respectful engagement and could endanger transgender students by exposing them to increased bullying and ostracization from their peers (see also GLAAD n.d.). As with lesbian, gay, bisexual, asexual, pansexual

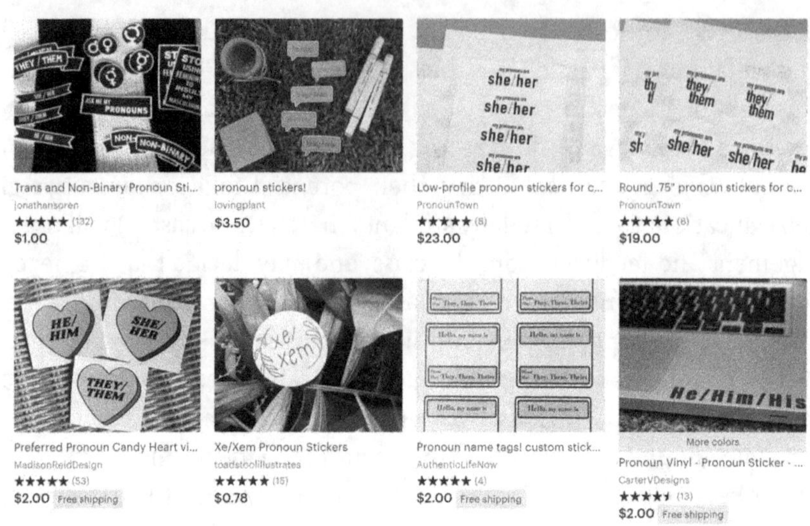

Figure 3.5 A sample of preferred pronoun stickers from various shops on the Etsy platform.

Retrieved from www.etsy.com/market/pronoun_stickers (image used under 17 USC § 107)

students, transgender students should be granted the dignity to come out if and when they choose. Our job as educators is only to create safe and respectful environments that do not replicate the marginalizing linguistic and cultural practices of the broader society in which we operate.

Use Local Queer Voices to Generate Interest and Relevance

Another way to queer practice is by bringing in, whenever possible, queer voices from the local community. I readily acknowledge that this may be challenging, or in some contexts impossible. However, I feel that the effort is truly worth it as it can have multiple benefits. First, it creates real-world LGBTQ+ representation in the classroom, allowing LGBTQ+-identified students to see themselves reflected in the classroom space in tangible, knowable, and immediately accessible ways. Second, it shows that LGBTQ+ lives and bodies take on a myriad of forms, not just the traditionally very limited ones seen in popular media through shows like *The Fosters, Modern Family, Queer Eye,* etc. These shows, while groundbreaking, have been variously accused of either whitewashing queer lives, rendering them handy plot devices to explain other character's trauma, or providing reductive views of what it means to be gay or lesbian in modern society (Waggoner 2018; cf. Craig, McInroy, McCready, and Alaggia 2015). Third, inviting guest speakers from local LGBTQ+ community shows students that LGBTQ+ people exist in their communities and are already part of their daily lives. That is, lesbians, gays, bisexuals, transgender, gender fluid, queer, asexual people are already present around them, perhaps in invisible ways. Moreover, many of these people have similar wants, needs and desires—physical security, legal recognition, job security, professional success, family stability, and so on—as the students themselves. Seeing these individuals and hearing from them helps to demystify LGBTQ+ lives in a very salient and very powerful way (see Curran 2002, 2006). Finally, it can help to redress one of the most endemic concerns voiced by straight-identified educators about queering their practice—specifically, that they don't know enough about LGBTQ+ lives, issues, and language to meaningfully include them in their teaching (Curran 2006; MacDonald, El-Metoui, Baynham, and Gray 2014; Rodriguez and Pinar 2007). This brings us quite nicely to the next practice-based change you can make to trouble normative classroom spaces.

Explore LGBTQ+ Issues with Your Students

Related to the point above, I strongly encourage practitioners to take the idea of queer pedagogy as it was outlined in the previous chapter to heart. Not only should we seek to trouble normative views of sexuality in our classroom spaces, but also normative views of education. Traditionally, our students have viewed us as authority figures in their social settings and have an erroneous view of us as experts in the sense that we know 'everything' about our chosen area (see Chory and Offstein 2016; Lacina 2002). This incorrect assumption often means that students are put off when we do not know something. I believe that a queer pedagogy allows us to better highlight the emergent nature of expertise and knowledge for our students by creating space for us to engage in inquiry and exploration with them. That is, it allows us to show our students the value in *not knowing*. It shows them that a gap in our knowledge, and awareness of it, creates space for inquiry and research; that it creates space for us to become more expert. It also allows us to model respectful engagement with our students through our approach to addressing gaps in our knowledge. So, while MacDonald (2015) reported many teachers feel uncomfortable with introducing LGBTQ+ issues because of their lack of knowledge, I want to encourage you to embrace this and make it part of the way that you trouble the classroom as a normative space. Make it clear to your students that you do not know everything about this topic and that you are going to explore together. Turn the moment of not knowing into a valuable tool of joint discovery and a chance to trouble the normative educational discourse that we must know everything all the time. Use the moment to create value around uncertainty and the acknowledgements of the limits of our knowledge. This can be a powerful moment for our students and also help them to begin reformulating their views of educational success and the breadths and limits of expertise more generally.

Take a Queer Approach to Language

Another route through which to trouble normative classrooms is to take a queer approach to language. Here, advances from World English, a sub-field of sociolinguistics, can be particularly helpful (see B. Kachru 2006; Kachru and Nelson 2006). World Englishes describes the spread of the English language through the (neo-)colonial efforts of the United Kingdom and the United States, paying particular attention to how English remained and evolved once the colonizer retreated. The World Englishes framework provides us with tools to describe locally relevant new Englishes, such as Indian English, Sri Lankan English, Singaporean English (Singlish), and so on. Moreover, it allows us to celebrate the properties of these local varieties and their unique abilities to reflect lived experiences in these new contexts, to push back against native speaker bias, and to find new positions from which to view language proficiency. Moreover, there is a rich body of queer contact literatures—novels, essays, poems—written in local Englishes that can be used in the classroom to queer course readings and normative views towards language and sexuality (see Tawake 2006; Paiz, Comeau, Zhu, Zhang and Santiano, 2018). Using queer contact literatures can also have the added benefit of highlighting non-Western LGBTQ+ identities for students, further tearing down normative views of sexuality (see Liu 2015).

Deploying advances from World Englishes is an option that I feel is particularly salient in ELT contexts because of our explicit focus on the forms language. Admittedly, it is one that takes different forms in traditionally defined ESL and EFL context. In the ESL context, such as teaching at a

British or an Australian university, the focus and the goals shifts towards creating increased value around multilingual abilities and hybrid forms of language, what Canagarajah (2013) refers to as translingual abilities. In the EFL context, it creates space to engage with non-Western varieties of English and to challenge normative attitudes towards what constitutes proficiency and fluency in a language. It decentres the English language and creates space for non-Western, local varieties of English to become the desired target, as opposed to chasing the moving target that is speaking like a so-called native speaker.

Conclusion

In this chapter, I have worked to describe the properties of normative classroom settings and the potential negative impacts of them on learners, especially ones that may identify as LGBTQ+. It is essential to keep in mind that we must be ever vigilant about the ways that normativity can creep into our classes. This requires us occasionally to take a critical eye to our practice and to the physical space in which we teach. The opening of this chapter outlined the ways that classes may help to reinforce heteronormative discourses. It is also, therefore, vital that we keep an eye on how our attempts to create LGBTQ+-inclusive educational spaces may work also to reinforce *homonormative* discourses, which Duggan (2002) and Liu (2015) have defined as the view that only certain homosexualities—typically creative, affluent and usually white ones—are socially acceptable, valued, and valid. For example, if we alter our classroom decorations to feature LGBTQ+ activists, artist, and cultural figures, we must take a further step back and ask whether or not we are including voices and bodies from the global margins. Are people of colour and differing physical ability also represented? Or, are we inadvertently whitewashing queerness for our students. This concern is why I, and other Queer TESOLers and applied linguists advocate for a queer inquiry that is more than just watching episodes of sitcoms that feature LGBTQ+ characters or plot lines.

Key Takeaways

This chapter also offered some concrete advice on how to begin using your teaching practice to begin pushing back against heteronormative social discourses. It also highlighted how this push against normativity—how the act of queering the classroom—is about more than just sexual identity. It requires us also to interrogate and tear down other normativities, such as the normative view of the teacher as expert, as the holder of all of the answers. Queer pedagogies require us to acknowledge the limits of our own knowledge and to engage in joint discovery and knowledge creation with our students. To that end, I want to leave you with five key takeaways from this chapter.

- Normativity creeps into our educational spaces in somewhat surprising ways, from physical layout to seemingly innocuous décor decisions. This requires us to be vigilant for ways that we can trouble these decisions to create a more inclusive environment for all learners.

- It is essential to avoid the 'inoculation' or 'one-and-done' approach to queering classroom practice. Do not have a 'gay day', leave that to the amusement parks. Instead, to truly queer our classroom practice, we must look for ways to incorporate LGBTQ+ content and voices throughout the curriculum and to do so in ways that move beyond the traditional discussions on family, gender, and romance, and that take place outside of reading/writing or speaking/listening classes.

- Queering our educational spaces requires us to make joint inquiry a regular part of our classroom practice. Too often, straight and LGBTQ+ educators alike worry that they 'don't know enough' about LGBTQ+ issues or how to present them to their students in linguistically and ethically appropriate ways. Great! Investigate with your students and show them that being an expert means knowing how to explore possibilities and to look for answers across numerous sources of information.

- Building inclusive classroom spaces also mean taking a queer view towards language and laying bear and troubling the ways that monolingualism and native speakerism comes to reinforce normative views about who has access to and voice in the English language. This often means creating space for global varieties of English in the classroom and creating value around multilingual voices and resources.

- Finally, troubling normative classroom practices requires us to be ever reflexive in our practices. It is not enough to incorporate queer pedagogies into our practice and to add LGBTQ+ representative décor, lessons, and realia. We must also keep an eye on how our efforts to be more inclusive of LGBTQ+ voices may reinforce Eurocentric and classist views of the LGBTQ+ community, ignoring its considerable global diversity.

Reflexive Practice Prompt

To help stimulate your reflection on the topics discussed in this chapter, you can make use of the following questions:

- How does my physical classroom potentially contribute to a normative environment? What is in my control to change?
- What small changes can I make to my lesson planning and course theme to make it more inclusive of LGBTQ+ voices and topics?
- How can I create an environment of joint discovery with my students to trouble their normative views of expertise and to create value around critical inquiry?
- How can I bring in global voices and non-Western varieties of English to trouble normative discourses about language and proficiency? How can I create value around multilingual voices and resources?

4

Troubling Normative Curricular Materials

AT A GLANCE

Introduction

With a better understanding of how heteronormativity may creep into our classrooms and our practices, it is now time to turn our attention to curricular materials. Past research has shown rather resoundingly that much of the material that we bring to class with us to support our teaching—things like textbooks, extensive readers, worksheets, assignment prompts, assessments, and so on—reflect heteronormative worldviews (see Erlman 2015; Gray 2013; Paiz 2015). Moreover, many students view curricular materials to be dependable representations of cultural norms/values and language use (see Mustapha 2013). While educational materials may seem like a low-stakes concern, they are powerful, salient representations of a target culture's perceived values and the identity options that are available to language learners (see Paiz 2015b, 2019; Shardakova and Pavlenko 2004). Not only are textbooks authoritative representations to learners, but they are also an essential educational aide to teachers—both novice and expert—because they can scaffold lesson planning and reinforce key learning objectives (Ball and Feiman-Menser 1988). When we stop to consider how time is often at a premium for many ELT professionals—whether K-12 educators, private sector instructors, or adjunct/contract professors—the importance of mainstream, published curricular materials becomes all the more salient.

Given the vital role of textbooks and other curricular materials, it is essential to consider how to integrate them into an LGBTQ+-inclusive classroom, especially when the vast majority of commercially available materials remain consistently heteronormative in their reflection of society (Gray 2013; Paiz 2015a). Here is where the queer inquiry-based pedagogical approach advocated for in the last two chapters can become particularly useful as you attempt to ameliorate the effects that these normative texts might have in your educational spaces. To make the connection between queer inquiry-based pedagogy and curricular materials clearer, this chapter will begin by outlining the myriad issues presented by the use of normative curricular materials and their impact on our students. This will include a description of normative materials and an explanation for why so many mainstream materials reflect heteronormative values. Then, this chapter will move on to discussing various ways that you can address the issues presented by normative materials by providing you with specific strategies for both queering commercially available materials and for developing your own. The chapter closes out by providing some advice on deploying and revising queered curricular materials.

The Problems with Normative Materials

Throughout this chapter, curricular materials will refer to the texts, textbooks, handouts, worksheets, PowerPoint decks, YouTube videos, etc. that we use to extend and scaffold our classroom teaching. A key difference between texts and textbooks is that textbooks are purpose-built for use in educational contexts and often combine instructional material with learning support tips and reinforcement exercises, while texts are extensive readers that may or may not have been created specifically for the classroom. Irrespective of the kind of curricular material that we chose to focus on there are three givens that we can safely assume: (1) these materials, especially commercially available ones, almost always reflect heteronormative, cisnormative, and ableist world views (see Gray 2013; Paiz 2015a; Shardakova and Pavlenko 2004); (2) the reality of the preceding assumption is unlikely to change because of the conservative nature of textbook publishers (Apple and Christian-Smith 1991; Paiz 2015a); and, (3) commercially available, mass-market curricular materials are essential scaffolds for educators—both ones that are early service and that are established practitioners (Collopy 2003; Nicol and Crespo 2006; Richards 2001). Given this fact, and that students see them as important tools to facilitate learning (see De Vincenti, Giovanangeli, and Ward 2007), we cannot underestimate their potential impacts on our teaching, on our classrooms, and on how our students come to view the target language, cultures, and values.

This, of course, means that we must be cognizant to the potential negative impacts of curricular materials that reify a heteronormative world view. Moreover, remember that normative resources are everywhere. In earlier research, both Gray (2013) and I showed that most of the items in our samples of ESL/EFL textbooks reflected heteronormative orientations because of how they chose to either include or, more commonly, exclude LGBTQ+ narratives, characters, and topics (see also Paiz 2015a). In a sample of 45 ESL reading texts and textbooks, I found that all but two items were dominantly heteronormative in their representation of mainstream Western society. Even more troubling is that when language textbooks do often include LGBTQ+ content, it does so in ways that either fetishize it by making it merely a subject of debate or by presenting LGBTQ+ individuals as diseased or socially maligned and malignant (see De Vincenti, Giovanangeli, and Ward 2007).

This negative representation of LGBTQ+ bodies and lives creates an environment that contributes to the replication of heteronormative discourses by showing our students that only cisgender, straight lives matter and are valued in English-speaking societies. This means that for our students to imagine themselves in our classrooms, they must envision a cisgender, straight identity, as anything else will marginalize them in a classroom space that is supposed to be supportive and inclusive (see Shardakova and Pavlenko 2004). By ignoring LGBTQ+ voices and bodies, heteronormative curricular materials make it so that our students, regardless of their actual sexual or gender identities, feel compelled to take on a cisgender, straight identity if they want to fit into the imagined world of the native speaker as it is presented to them in course materials (Kanno 2003; Pavlenko and Norton 2007). Speaking to the power of these imagined identities in the language learning context, Pavlenko (2001) underscored how seeing oneself as part of a broader communicative community—participatory, integrated, and welcomed—played a crucial role in students' overall progress and perseverance as language learners.

Moreover, curricular materials serve a vital support role for practitioners of all backgrounds, but even more so for early-service practitioners. As mentioned previously, the research continues to show that early-service educators tend to rely on textbooks and other pre-made curricular materials, both commercial and open access, to help with tasks such as lesson planning, assignment design and scaffolding, assessment, and so on (see Richards 2001; Ball and Feiman-Menser 1988). This means that publicly available materials, whether commercially available like *LEAP Advanced* from Pearson Education ESL (Beatty 2013) or open access ones like those available through OER Commons (www.oercommons.org/browse?f.keyword=esl), hold the potential for considerable influence over ELT interventions. Take, for example, the early-service educator who is teaching a new course for the first time. At this stage in their career, these individuals have emergent teaching philosophies and classroom practices; that is, they are still discovering their voice and professional selves (see Deters 2011). To help fill in gaps in their knowledge or experience, and to ensure that minimal instructional needs are met, they may rely on published curricular materials to a higher degree than their more experienced peers.

Moreover, they may be less likely to actively problematize these materials because they are either time-strapped, needing an immediate solution to a pedagogical problem, or because they have not yet had the time to reflect on the material and its use in their classrooms. Our students, however, seriously engage with this material—even if we, their teachers, are only in the process of testing it out. So, our students see it as a reflection of acceptable language use, social interaction, and worldviews of the target culture. Taken together, this contributes to the reification of heteronormative discourses in our classrooms.

It should be noted, however, that the same can happen for seasoned teachers who are facing heavy workloads, because published materials allow us to offload a part of our prep work on to the textbooks or web-based educational resources thereby allowing us to focus on other kinds of labour (e.g. grading, meeting with parents, committee work, etc.). Therefore, if we do not build in time to reflect on the materials that we use, or if we are not encouraged to do so by institutional or programmatic policy, it is easy for these materials that scaffold our teaching to become a crystallized part of our educator's toolkit and for their normative influence with students to be perpetuated across cohorts each year. So, when we uncritically use the chapter in the textbook on family relationships, we are signalling to our students that in our classrooms and English-speaking society only heterosexual, nuclear, families are *real* families and any other arrangement is something else, something less than.

The ways that our curricular materials reflect heteronormative discourses and their values are numerous—ranging from very explicit to very subtle. However, they all can have profound impacts on contributing to heteronormative practices and educational spaces, ones that leave our sexual and gender minority students feeling marginalized, out of place, and without a voice. To help reinforce this point, I will now provide brief analyses of three examples of heteronormative ELT materials. These examples will range from explicitly to surprisingly heteronormative, explanations of each category will be provided in the following sections. While these examples come from open educational resources (OERs), they mirror very closely the same moves that we see being made in heteronormative materials that are commercially available and mass produced (see Paiz 2015a).

Explicitly Heteronormative Materials

Explicitly heteronormative materials are those materials that either expressly state that heterosexuality is the only acceptable way of life, or that strongly seem to suggest it through repeatedly referencing only heterosexual relationships throughout the entire text. In an earlier study, I showed that this kind of explicit heteronormativity often happens in units on the family or in extensive readers that focus on dating and relationships, such as Leather's (2003) *Bad Love* or Hancock's (2008) *Love in the Lakes* (Paiz 2015a). In both of these extensive readers from Cambridge University Press, the focus is solely on heterosexual romances, even the 'bad romance' of Leather (2003) is in dating a rebellious boy that does not conform to the female protagonist's family's view of a good boyfriend. Moreover, the heteronormativity

Figure 4.1 Cover image from Cambridge University Press's *Love in the Lakes.*

Image used with permission

reflected in these materials is often perpetuated through illustrations in the book and cover art, as seen in Figure 4.1.

Explicitly heteronormative texts most often function by making it appear that only heterosexual relationships are valid, valued, and permissible in the target culture. Explicit heteronormativity can also occur through repeated references to only heterosexual couples throughout a text. This repeated reference serves to continually reinforce for the student the idea that only heterosexual lives exist in the target culture, and it works through the almost deliberate omission of LGBTQ+ lives and bodies. Take Krause's (2018) OER book *Home and School: Ten Easy Picture Stories for Beginning Students of English*. Three of the ten stories mention couples, particularly married couples. Moreover, each of these stories only indexes heterosexual couplings through explicit mentions in the text to husband/wife pairings (see Figure 4.2).

Subtly Heteronormative Materials

Texts that are *subtly heteronormative* may make no mention to heterosexual pairings, opting instead to use gender-neutral makers such as 'spouse'

Sunee and Chet live in an apartment

Figure 4.2 Story images from *Home and School* depicting heteronormative relationships.

Source: Krause (2018: 23–24, 31). Image used under creative commons 4.0 attribution licence

or 'partner' any time that they index a romantic or marital relationship. While moving towards being inclusive, this linguistic move is often coupled with graphical elements that only feature heterosexual couples, such as in Brenner, Ford, and Sullivan's (2007) *Celebrate! Holidays in the USA* produced and distributed by Office of English Language Programs under the auspices of the United States Department of State. In a short essay on birthdays and anniversaries, the text only references 'married couples' in text (ibid.: 103), but the only accompanying graphical element is a full-page, full-colour image of an elderly, white man and woman sitting in front of yellow cake with two lit candles in the shape of the number '50' (ibid.: 102). This coupling of gender-neutral, ostensibly inclusive language, with an image of a straight couple works to more subtly reinforce heteronormative social discourses through an unequal tension between text and image. Often, it is the image, which carries more rhetorical weight with the reader, that wins out as the reader seeks to use the multimodal input of the text to construct socially situated meaning (see Hassett and Schieble 2010). This means that even well-intentioned texts that opt for a more neutral approach can reinforce heteronormativity in our classes.

Surprisingly Heteronormative Materials

Occasionally, even curricular materials that we use because we believe that they directly subvert heteronormative discourses can end up reinforcing hetero- and homonormative ideologies. These *surprisingly heteronormative materials* share some of the following properties. They (a) typically represent LGBTQ+ issues as grounds for debate; (b) reduce LGBTQ+ issues to 'gay' issues, thereby ignoring the diversity in queer lives and experiences; (c) encourage students to consider LGBTQ+ lives, bodies, and desires as merely extensions of heterosexual ones by relying on what Duggan (2002) refers to as homonormativity; or (d) make it appear that LGBTQ+ topics are sensational ones because they either only reference celebrities or the health and legal challenges facings LGBTQ+ communities across the globe (see Paiz 2019; Motschenbacher and Stegu 2013).

Take, for example, the exercise provided in Banville (2017), which focuses on 'gay rights'. The exercise takes the form of a series of questions that students should ask each other about gay rights, their understanding of them, their knowledge of local gay rights, and their experience with gay rights conversations in their home countries. While a potentially good starting point, this exercise can reflect heteronormative and homonormative discourses in rather unexpected ways. For example, questions 9 and 10 for Student A to ask, 'What do you think of same-sex relations and the raising of children?' and 'Is marriage a relationship between only a man and woman' (Banville 2017). These two questions occurring in rapid succession primes students to consider the end goal of gay rights, at least as it is presented in this exercise, to be monogamous, child-rearing, marriage for members of the LGBTQ+ community, particularly for gay men and lesbians. This reinforces a homonormative discourse of 'us gays, we're just like you straights' that is deeply tied to heteronormative ideologies about marriage, family, and procreation (see Duggan 2002; Stryker 2008). Moreover, this excises also reinforces heteronormative discourses by potentially casting LGBTQ+ concerns as Western concerns by asking questions like 'Which nationalities do you think are the most homophobic?' (Banville 2017). Taken together, these kinds of questions, their wording, and their ordering all work to reinforce normative discourses in somewhat surprising ways, especially when there is a lack of support materials for educators who chose to use these curricular materials.

Redressing Normative Curricular Materials

With a better understanding of what heteronormative materials might look like, it is now time to turn our focus to how to address the problems presented by these kinds of resources when we encounter them or are required to use them in our teaching. To aid in this conversation, I want to begin by directly addressing pre-made curricular materials—things like extensive readers, textbooks, and other OERs—and offering some actionable strategies for making these often-normative materials more inclusive. Then, I will share some recommendations on developing your own inclusive curricular materials using the queer inquiry-based framework that was discussed in chapter two. Before continuing, however, it is important to keep in mind that troubling normativity in our curricular materials is an ongoing process and one on which we must reflect on our efforts from time to time (see 'Deploying Queer Materials' below).

Be Prepared with Supplemental Materials

Perhaps the primary tool at your disposal is coming to class prepared with supplemental materials that you can deploy alongside existing curricular materials. Admittedly, this requires advanced planning and knowledge of the resources available to find quality LGBTQ+-inclusive material. And, here we arrive at a major challenge for the modern educator. Except for a very small sub-set of university educators, many full-time ELT professionals, myself included, face heavy teaching loads in high-contact, intensive classes (see Kubota and Sun 2013). Couple this fact with the high number of part-time, adjunct professionals in TESOL, and you have a group of caring, professional educators with very little time on their hands to hunt for additional teaching resources. Moreover, while there is currently no clearinghouse for LGBTQ+ inclusive materials, there are organizations (such as GLSEN and the HRC's Welcoming Schools Initiative) that have begun compiling resource kits for educators, albeit they assume mainstream, native speaker classes. To begin addressing this issue, I will include references, and where possible links, to specific tools that you can use to help find supplemental materials. That being said, there are two essential questions that we must ask as we seek to trouble normative materials:

1 How do I know when I should bring in supplemental materials?

2 What kinds of materials should I consider using?

To explore the answers to these questions, I will use examples from popular ELT reading/writing and speaking/listening textbooks.

Hartmann and Blass's (2007) *Quest Intro: Reading and Writing* series is a popular commercial textbook in many EAP contexts because it covers a range of academic literacy skills while also exposing students to scaffolded academic discourse designed to be of interest to the students. In the intro level book of the series, there are a handful of readings that address various stereotypes, which would seem promising because of their potential to push against normative discourses. For example, the reading on children, gender, and toys summarizes recent psychology studies on how young boys and girls are socialized into their respective gender roles. It even recommends that parents should be encouraged to buy their children toys that are typically played with by the opposite gender. However, it does not provide any detail on how playing with a "girl's toy' [can] help him (a son) prepare for future relationships' (Hartmann and Blass 2007: 119–120), nor are there any activities in the text that are designed to get students thinking about this advice more critically. Therefore, even this well-intentioned text can end up reifying normative discourses about gender and sexuality. It does so by merely suggesting what the students may see as non-normative behaviours without creating space for students and educators to discuss the implications of this view or how the desired outcomes can be achieved in a way that meaningfully challenges the normative gender/sexual stereotypes that the reading is trying to push against. This may lead some students to disparage boys that play with girls toys as 'gay' (see also Moita-Lopes 2006).

To queer this reading further, it may be paired with an exercise like 'That's a (Gender) Stereotype' (GLSEN n.d.) or 'What are Gender Stereotypes' (Teaching Tolerance n.d.). Particularly helpful is that both of these exercises extend the existing materials in ways that can support English language students by including scaffolds like words lists that explain key terms in more accessible language and by directly addressing LGBTQ+ concerns such as gender expression, gender fluidity, and how stereotypes about gender and sexuality may often intersect. Alternatively, you could bring in level appropriate real-world materials, for example,

Hogan's (2018) *Detroit Free Press* article on legal challenges to gendered toys in fast food for children or Chack's (2014) list of products that are marketed at a specific gender group when the item does not need to be gendered in the first place. Bringing in these real-world items reinforces concepts from the primary reading while also extending in a direction that can be used to trouble normative views towards gender and sexuality.

Have Inclusive Activities Planned

If you have no control over the texts/textbooks that get used in your class, or if you do not have enough free time to hunt down and adapt online material to meet your needs, you can plan to deploy LGBTQ+-inclusive activities to augment the more normative readings and textbook activities. These activities can take many forms depending on available time, linguistic proficiency, goals of the course, and so no.

For example, elsewhere I have discussed the use of narrative illustration activities as powerful tools to help uncover the heteronormative assumptions that our students and we may make about the world around us (see Paiz 2020b). In these narrative illustration activities, students are provided with a 1–3-page, proficiency-keyed short story and must illustrate a central passage from the story. These stories all have LGBTQ+ themes but use gender-neutral language and rhetorical ambiguity that require students to have particular cultural knowledge and ideological orientations to decode them thoroughly. Therefore, in many drawings that the students produce, their assumptions about race, gender, and sexual identity come out and become the starting point for in-class conversations about language and our preconceptions about things like sexual identity.

Another powerful tool is simulation games for language learning and communication practice. Simulations can be particularly useful in English for Specific Purposes (ESP) classes that focus on intercultural communication in the workplace. Simulations, or sims for short, are structured communicative events that are tied to specific learning outcomes, during which the communication is functionally real and tied to a specific goal (e.g. getting across an unfamiliar town, uncovering patient history, etc.; Jones 1982; Coleman and Yamazaki 2018). During sims, student encounter communicative environments that are closely modelled on the real world. So, if a student is in a simulation where they are ordering food at a restaurant, the classroom will be set up to mirror either a fast food, fast/casual, or fine dining space, with some students taking the roles of the wait staff and others of patrons. Additionally, the communication is functionally real, with participants needing to produce language as they would if they were really in the context. The functional reality of language in a sim means that communicative breakdowns have real consequence (e.g. not getting what you ordered; not prescribing the right medication, etc.). Finally, sims are highly structured to help guide learners through the experience and to uncover the important learning points once the simulation ends (Jones 1982).

Simulations can also be used to make the ESL/EFL classroom more LGBTQ+ inclusive. Muckler, Leonard, and Cicero (2019) describe a training simulation that they use in medical schools to increase students' awareness of transgender issues, ethical care, and respectful language. In their sim, participants took turns taking on the roles of nurses and trans patients during a pre-anaesthesiology consultation. The students were tasked with respectfully engaging with one another to uncover current medications and other medical histories, the sharing of which may out the patient participant as transgender (Muckler, Leonard, and Cicero 2019: 45-46). This simulation is one that could be easily modified for an ESP course by beginning with a briefing on trans-inclusive language and discussions on engaging respectfully with LGBTQ+ individuals. During the briefing, specific linguistic items and rhetorical moves would be presented by the teacher and discussed to ensure clarity. Then, during the simulation, the students would attempt to deploy what they have learned in a sheltered, but functionally real, communicative encounter. Afterwards, the teacher would use their observations from during the simulation to lead a debriefing that highlights both communicative successes and failures while uncovering persistent misunderstandings and sharing strategies for future communicative success.

Use Other Instructional Tools to Scaffold and Queer Heteronormative Materials

Another option is to use the other instructional tools at your disposal to present students with non-heteronormative examples and materials. For example, you might use a PowerPoint slide like the one in Figure 4.3. This image shows a slide that has been used in a basic ESL tutorial on families, and it draws direct attention to some of the different forms that families can take by including both gay male and lesbian families, one of which is also a mixed-race couple. In the original presentation, students had to read a textbook chapter on families before coming to the workshop. The chapter presented the English names for different family members and an explanation of their relationships (Carlson 2018).

To help supplement the instruction, the workshop facilitator created this slide using open-access images that were available through Wikimedia.org and allowed for commercial use and remixing. During the workshop, the facilitator pointed out that families can take other shapes beyond the ones discussed in the textbook and showed the image in figure 8, below. Afterwards, the facilitator asked students to take time to map their families using a rough family tree-like structure, which was then used to lead a discussion on lived experiences with family configurations.

Other instructional tools may include items such as classroom posters and instructional design elements around the classroom. For example,

Families Can Take a lot of Shapes

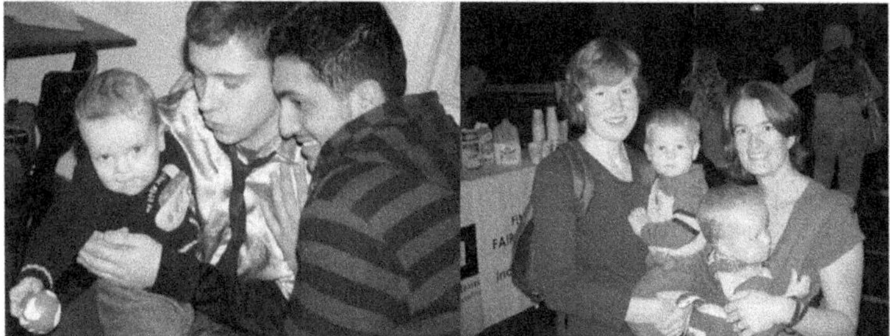

Figure 4.3 PowerPoint slide featuring LGBTQ+ families.

Source: Image all rights the author. Pictures on slide used under Creative Commons 4.0 attribution licence (Wikimedia Commons)

some classes may include posters and infographics about respectful relationships and dealing with relationship abuse while working through units on dating and relationships.[1] In many cases, these kinds of classroom posters serve an instructional purpose, in that they provide class-related information to students, but they often include heteronormative presentations in the form of only having heterosexual statistics reported or only using heterosexual iconography in depicting relationship pairings. These posters can serve to reinforce the notion that only heterosexuality is valid and valued, especially for the linguistically and culturally diverse students who may find themselves in a mainstream, K-12 health class. So, including infographics from organizations like Teaching Tolerance (teachingtolerance.org), GLSEN (glsen.org), or Facing History and Ourselves (facinghistory.org) can help to include LGBTQ+ voices and to shed light on queer concerns while also equipping L2 English students with the language and information necessary to discuss relationships and sexual health in linguistically appropriate, LGBTQ+-inclusive ways.

Bring in Community Partners and Realia

Another option for combating the effects of heteronormative texts is to follow the example in Ó'Móchain (2006) and to partner with LGBTQ+ individuals and organizations in the local community to bring in guest speakers and community-related realia. A good example of a time to bring in local community partners is during career days. Inviting in LGBTQ+-identified EMTs, teachers, dentists, engineers, and clergy can highlight the diverse career options that successful LGBTQ+ professionals can take. It can also push back against normative discourses that suggest that LGBTQ+ individuals are best suited for creative careers like professional dance, hair styling, and interior design. Moreover, it creates space for students to learn about the unique challenges that can be faced by LGBTQ+ professionals. Doing so can help provide exposure to the language necessary to respectfully engage with LGBTQ+ populations and to advocate for students to advocate for themselves and others. This can be facilitated by planning out questions to ask of all guest speakers about their jobs such as the following:

- How did you decide on your career?
- What special training did you need for your job?

- What do like about your job?
- What challenges do you face in your job?
- What do you do if people think you can't/don't do the kind of work that you do?

This final question can uncover answers that may be of interest to linguistically and culturally diverse students. For example, a lesbian, Hispanic professor from the local university may share an experience where she was confused for a secretary or where a colleague thought she did not need maternity leave because they felt that lesbian couples should not have children (for similar stories, see Equality Challenge Unit 2015). These stories can help raise student awareness about the challenges faced by LGBTQ+ professionals and help them to understand better the need to advocate for our LGBTQ+-identified friends and peers.

Another option is to look for opportunities to bring in LGBTQ+-themed realia to help support curricular materials and to make lessons more inclusive. For example, in a class that has a civics focus, the teacher could bring in flags from the LGBTQ+ community when discussing locally relevant symbols, which may more traditionally include national, state/prefectural/county, and local flags and seals. The LGBTQ+ flags can be used to extend classroom discussions about how flags and seals are used to help build local identities and function as powerful community symbols. So, in the case of the United States, we might discuss the meaning behind the colours of the US flag or the heraldic banner that makes up the US state flag of Maryland. We can then extend these lessons to discuss the meaning behind the colours of the LGBTQ+ and Transgender pride flags, underscoring the importance of these symbols as identity markers and how they often travel beyond official functions to become commercialized as bumper stickers and bookmarks that further extend their identity functions.

Model and Deploy Critical Close Readings

Another option available to you is to engage in a critical close reading of course texts with your students. Very often we tend to consume assigned readings and textbook passages and activities for the content that they present and how they tie to course learning objectives or assignment requirements before moving on to the next unit. Certain structural constraints encourage this behaviour—such as preparing for a standardized examination, the need to move students through units of instruction to prepare them for matriculation to mainstream classes, and so on. However, taking a moment to model and deploy critical close readings of the commercially available classroom materials that we use in our classes—whether by choice or requirement—can be very helpful for our students. To begin with, it forces students to slow down and seriously engage with the language and rhetoric of the texts that we are using. It shows them how to consider the interplay between text, context, and images to consider how we make meaning from what we read. Moreover, by modelling *critical* close reading for our students and making it a part of a regular practice, we aid our students in acquiring the critical thinking skills that are valued in many educational contexts in the global West (see Atkinson 1997).

For example, in an intermediate reading/writing class in an intensive English programme, we might assign extensive reading for our students. Often, this takes the form of a short novel graduate reader, such as the *Doctor Who* readers available through Pearson ELT or the post-apocalyptic romance *Not Without You* available through Oxford University Press. To engage in a more critical close readings, we would begin to ask questions like:

- What relationships do we see represented in the text?
- What do we notice about the structure of these relationships as it related to gender, age, race, etc.?
- What does this suggest to us about what the text values?
- How are these views supported by the graphic elements of the text?
- Do the pictures that go with the text reinforce these ideas or others?
- Who is ignored by this view? Who is given preference?
- What would alternatives look like?

By deploying questions like these in our reading, or by focusing on two or three of them during group readings, we show our students how to engage with the text critically and to begin uncovering normative stances that may be reflected to them in it. When we make this kind of activity a regular part of our practice, we show that this kind of engagement with a text is essential to understanding not only its meaning but also its social relevance. Moreover, we expose the students to habits of mind that allow them to uncover normativity on their own in future classes; and, we equip them with the linguistic and rhetorical skills necessary to respectfully engage in conversations about these matters that they might have in future conversations both in and out of the classroom.

Each of the strategies discussed above provides us with the necessary pedagogical tools to take problematic resources, ones that reify heteronormative worldviews, and to make them work more inclusively. No matter what mix of strategies you choose to deploy, there are a few points to keep in mind that will help make them more effective. First, and foremost, always invite student perspectives, experiences, and voices into the process. Create space for student to contribute to your efforts to queer the classroom space and make it more inclusive. By purposefully making space for student voices, you help to further queer the classroom by troubling traditional, normative views of classroom roles and power dynamics. Moreover, you give yourself a sort of pedagogical springboard when it comes to queering heteronormative materials by having a ready access point for students and LGBTQ+-focused conversations. Second, always be on the lookout for normative worldviews in your curricular materials and work together with students to challenges these views. You should engage in this critical work with your students throughout the curriculum and be looking for normativity as it relates to gender, success, expertise, and so on. Do not focus solely on sexuality and sexual identity, as to do so is to fall short of the goals of queering ELT, which is to equip our students with the habits of mind and linguistics tools needed to problematize *all* normative discourses. Finally, keep in mind that you will be working to inculcate a spirit of restive problematizing in your classroom (see Pennycook 2001). By creating value around questioning the social fabrics in which we are implicated, we prepare our students to deploy their multilingual and multicultural resources to be more aware and capable global citizens (see Appiah 2007).

Deploying Queer Materials

While finding LGBTQ+-inclusive materials for L2 English students can be challenging, deploying them in our classes can be a downright nerve-racking experience. Concerns about how students will respond to LGBTQ+ content can give us plenty of reason for pause before deploying more inclusive materials (see Saunston 2018; Nelson 2006). Additionally, we may worry about being an ideologue and losing focus on the language teaching mission of ESL/EFL classes (Pandavar and Paiz 2017; Silva 1997). Moreover, one may have justified, exigent fears of how administrators and parents will react to the inclusion of LGBTQ+ content and materials in our English language classes. This fear can be amplified by being a contingent faculty member with fewer apparent protections than most full-time tenured/tenure-track professors and teachers. This means that greater care and planning must be used when preparing to deploy queer curricular material. Taking the time to consider how you will respond to pushback related to your use of LGBTQ+-inclusive materials can be helpful. Here, I will provide you with some tools for thoughts to help prepare you to successfully rollout LGBTQ+-inclusive curricular materials in your educational practice. As I have outlined elsewhere, part of what we must be prepared to do when we engage in queering the English language classroom is to negotiate its inclusion with our students, colleagues, administrators, and parents (see Paiz 2020a).

With students, this negotiation begins by giving them advanced notice that you will be taking a queered approach to your pedagogy throughout the semester. This can be done by introducing the term and explaining what it means. Alternatively, it can be done by sharing your statement of teaching philosophy at the beginning of the term and giving students a chance to ask questions about your teaching approach. The former is potentially more suited to primary and secondary settings, or to classes that target the lower end of the proficiency spectrum. The latter, on the other hand, may be better suited to advanced undergraduate and graduate courses. A crucial part of this move is to let your students know why you feel it is important to take an inclusive approach to teaching, perhaps by drawing connections between the marginalization of the LGBTQ+ community and immigrant communities and communities of colour. After showing students why including LGBTQ+ voices is essential, it is often helpful to draw clear connections between the material that you will use in class and how it helps to accomplish the learning objectives of the course. If a student pushes back, it may be helpful to invite the student to meet with you during office hours or after class so that you can have a serious and conscientious discussion about their concerns and your reasoning for building a classroom that is inclusive of all identities.

You may also face some pushback from peers and administrators when utilizing LGBTQ+-inclusive materials in your classes. I can distinctly recall a rather passionate conversation with a colleague at NYU Shanghai about just this topic. They were concerned about a heavy-handed and preachy approach to LGBTQ+ inclusion, while I wanted them to see how important it is to make space for marginalized identities. By the end of the conversation, neither of us changed our views. Since these kinds of conversation are likely to come up when our institutional others find out about our use of LGBTQ+ content, it is important to be prepared for these conversations. As a starting point, it is best to be prepared to tie your use of LGBTQ+-inclusive materials and pedagogies to broader curricular needs and institutional mission and goals. By having talking points prepared ahead of time, you will be better positioned for any conversations with critical stakeholders. Additionally, it models for administrators and peers how to talk about your approach with other stakeholders (e.g. parents, accrediting bodies, external reviewers, etc.). In conversations with colleagues and administration, it can also be helpful to link your use of queer materials to diversity, equity, and inclusion more generally. Doing so creates currency around your use of a queer pedagogical approach and the LGBTQ+-inclusive materials that go with it. Moreover, it situates your efforts in a key moment facing education and allows you to bring in relevant research and scholarship to support your argument for more inclusive pedagogies. Finally, it may be useful to link up with partners both inside and outside of your institution to support you in these conversations. For example, connecting with the local affiliate of GLSEN can allow you to make use of their talking points and consultants as you prepare for these conversations. Alternatively, inviting in a local LGBTQ+ educational researcher can provide useful perspective and show that your approach is grounded in educational best practices.

Parents and guardians also represent a crucial stakeholder population, especially in K-12 settings. And, a quick review of headlines from the past five years show that they can often be vocal in their opposition to the inclusion of LGBTQ+ content on ideological, political, or religious grounds. Given the strength of parental voices in some K-12 settings, this has led to some apprehension on the part of teachers, which has been well attested in the literature (Ullman and Ferfolja 2016). Parents may also wonder why sexuality is coming up at all in an English language class. To help with parental responses to deploying LGBTQ+ content in classes, it is often useful to be prepared to show parents how creating an inclusive classroom space facilitates language acquisition processes by lowering affective barriers. Additionally, it speaks to students' acculturational needs for programmes located in Western contexts where LGBTQ+ issues are part of national discourses (Alexander 2008). Another strategy is to connect your use of queer materials to working with other marginalized groups, reminding parents of the importance of providing representation to as many social groups as we are able. That is, just as we want to see ourselves reflected in the world around us, our students need to see themselves and diverse others represented in their classroom materials. If the conversations are getting particularly heated, it may be beneficial to have a sympathetic administrative partner in place to take over those conversations, creating important critical distance for both you and the parent/guardian-stakeholders.

Conclusion

This chapter has focused on addressing the problems presented by heteronormative curricular materials—the extensive readers, course textbooks, assignment sheets, and the like—that we may deploy either by choice or by institutional mandate. Queering these resources requires us to be ever vigilant for the different ways that normative discourses come to be reflected in these materials. Therefore, we must engage in a restive problematizing of these educational materials to uncover ways that non-mainstream identities are marginalized, rendered invisible, and silenced. Moreover, we must remember to bear in mind that queering ELT materials requires us to consider more than just the lessons on romance, dating, and family. We must look for the fingerprints of normativity in all our lessons and in forms that move beyond just sexuality and sexual identity.

Key Takeaways

Addressing normativity in curricular materials is a rather tall order, but one that the strategies in this chapter have sought to help you address in your practice. Whether you choose to supplement required materials with community-based resources and guest speakers, or to engage in close readings and interrogations of texts with your students, queering the texts and textbooks that you use in your classroom can have profound positive effects for learners. First, it shows them that we, as educators and society, value diversity in more than just name. By actively creating space and representation of marginalized voices, we embrace diversity in all of its forms; we do not just use diversity as a selling point, but we leverage it as a collective strength. Second, it shows students that even if we do not readily see a marginalized individual in our classes, we must be prepared, linguistically and rhetorically, to speak out for their accesses and inclusion in our public spaces. Finally, queering our materials underscores for students the role that culture and national discourses play in language learning. As Alexander (2008) pointed out, being able to cogently and respectfully join into conversations about sexuality and sexual identity is an essential skill in modern literacy in the global West. However, this is not just a Western issue; it is a global one. LGBTQ+ communities and their advocates are speaking out across the globe for greater recognition and legal protection, from transgender/hajira rights in India (Sharma 2012) to LGBTQ+ marriage advocates in Taiwan (Aspinwall 2019) and the decriminalization of homosexuality in Kenya (Bearak 2019).

This chapter has also sought to provide you with guidance on what to do while deploying LGBTQ+ resources and the disparate conversations that will likely be had with students, peers, administrators, and parental stakeholders. While some of the advice may seem to presage an uphill battle through thick resistance, rest assured that the benefits of creating more inclusive classroom spaces cannot be ignored. In the next two chapters, I will provide additional insights that can drive your queered practice. Chapter 5 will focus on gauging reactions and negotiating resistance, while Chapter 6 will outline the educational and acculturational benefits of queered ELT pedagogies. By way of closing the current discussion, however, allows me to give one final piece of advice on queering your classroom materials. Just as with queering your classroom practice, this is not a 'one-and-done' proposition. Instead, it requires you to be open to feedback from students and professional peers and to reflect on the successes and failures of using the new materials—be open to revising these materials as your queer pedagogy evolves.

Reflexive Praxis Prompt

To help you consider how the discussion in this chapter might fit into your practice as an educator, consider these questions:

- Looking at the materials that I currently use in my classes (reading texts, textbooks, etc.), how do I see heteronormativity reflected in these materials?
- What are the constraints and affordances of my local context that may (de-)facilitate my attempts to make these materials more LGBTQ+-inclusive?
- Which strategies outlined in this chapter do I think will be most successful given my contextual constraints and affordances?
- What community partners might exist to facilitate my efforts to queer my classroom materials and to make them more inclusive?

5

Gauging Reactions and Addressing Challenges

AT A GLANCE

Introduction

Previous chapters have encouraged you to take a critical approach to whatever form of queer pedagogy that you choose to adopt. In this chapter, I will build on that recommendation with some specific actions that you can take as you attempt to maintain a critical view of your practice. Specifically, this chapter will focus on two central facets of maintaining criticality—collecting and acting on learner and peer feedback and navigating challenges to your use of a queer pedagogy. Both actions provide you with essential perspectives as you seek to revise your pedagogical approach to make it more relevant to the needs of your specific learner population. Moreover, gaining feedback from learners and peers may also help you to ensure that your deployment of a queer inquiry-informed pedagogy is helping learners to meet course/programme goals.

Additionally, navigating challenges to your attempts to make the English language classroom more LGBTQ+ inclusive can also be very helpful. While facing pushback from administrators, colleagues, students, or parents is most certainly daunting—being both affectively and cognitively draining—it provides you with another form of useful feedback that you can use to revise your queered pedagogical approach. Moreover, facing such resistance can equip you with the necessary coping strategies for the future and essential insights on how to navigate institutional and family-facing spaces by uncovering sticking points for various stakeholders as well as potentially unveiling key allies.

To that end, this chapter will first outline in greater detail what taking a critical approach entails, focusing on some central areas of pedagogy and materials that you should bear in mind. It will then provide you with guidance on collecting feedback from students at various points in your engagement with them before discussing what to do with the gathered data. This chapter will conclude by discussing the resistance that you may face in your attempts and how to navigate challenges that may arise from different stakeholder communities. A particular focus will be given to how you can turn your experiences with such opposition into meaningful, contextually relevant changes to your attempts to make your classroom more inclusive.

A Critical Approach to Queering the Classroom

Queer approaches to ELT are often situated as part of the constellation of critical approaches to applied linguistics and TESOL (see Hawkins and Norton 2009; Pennycook 2001). Therefore, we must turn a critical eye to them and our usage of them as part of our pedagogies. And, we must do so because there are many moving pieces to consider in the ecological setting that is our local context and how the English language classroom is situated in it. So, taking a critical approach to queering the language classroom allows us to meet the needs of our students better, and to speak to local lived experiences and LGBTQ+ lives and bodies. To that end, there are three main areas to consider as we work to take a critical view of our queered ELT practice: the self, the students, and the institution.

The Self

I have been working with queer approaches to ELT for just over five years by the time this book comes out, perhaps a couple of more by the time you read this—barring career change or early retirement. At first, it was a way for me to explore and make sense of my own sexual identity through a medium in which I was more comfortable—academic research and scholarship. Over that time, I have come to realize that reflecting critically on my practice as a queer educator, and on my attempts to make my classrooms more LGBTQ+-inclusive is a critical consideration. This realisation has been spurred on by my departmental colleagues, disciplinary peers, and the numerous question-askers that have attended my sessions at conferences. The reason that critical reflection is so crucial is because it is the only tool that we have to help us ensure that we (a) *are not* just functioning as classroom ideologues, (b) *are not* just seeking to 'convert' students to our way of thinking, and (c) *are* providing our students with as complete a representation of the diversity of LGBTQ+ experiences as we can. Allow me to briefly share three anecdotes from my advising, teaching, and educational consulting experience to help reinforce just how vital reflection might be.

While I was working in China, I had the honour of working with a group of students for whom LGBTQ+ equity and representation were very, very important. It was an energetic group that threw themselves rather wholeheartedly at the question of how to make our institution more LGBTQ+-inclusive and how to raise awareness of LGBTQ+ issues in the local community, which was a large, metropolitan community on the Eastern coast of China. Many of the students had read works like Sedgwick's (2008) *The Epistemology of the Closet* or Butler's (1990) *Gender Trouble: Feminism and the Subversion of Identity* and were eager to apply what they felt they had learned to this new context. What they ran up against, however, was that Western queer theory often does not travel as well as we would hope because global experiences of queerness are not universal (see Fraiberg, Wang, and You 2017; Khayatt 2003; Liu 2015). That is, local experiences with and expressions of queer bodies and lives differ wildly, so the carte blanche application of Western queer theory and identity politics can often fall flat. This is where I encouraged the students that came to me for advice to consider the voices that were informing their approach and to ask, 'what privileges and assumptions are shaping what this scholar has to say, or my own understanding of LGBTQ+ issues?' Only in doing so, in taking a step back, can we begin to see potential limits and prevent ourselves from becoming dogmatic adherents to an ideology attempting to facilitate its spread. Also, spreading an ideology is not the point of queering our educational practice. Instead, it is to create inclusive spaces that model respectful engagement with and advocacy for what are often dangerously marginalized populations.

This same group of students eventually invited me and one of my colleagues, a lesbian scholar of colour, to come talk to them about our differing opinions on LGBTQ+ issues in education (Pandavar and Paiz 2017). During this hour-and-a-half long debate, my colleague skilfully deployed rhetorical positionings to help advance her case. One of which was to voice concern that queering the classroom was a form of 'missionary work' seeking to sway hearts and minds over to LGBTQ+ causes. However, this is not the case. To echo Krause (2017), with ESL/EFL students, queering the classroom is not about winning over hearts and minds, rather it is about raising awareness and modelling respectful engagement. However, my colleague brings up a valuable point. To ensure that we are not just proselytizing to our students about the LGBTQ+ gospel of inclusion, we must critically reflect on our approach to queering the classroom. This begins by asking yourselves questions like, 'Am I creating a space for respectful engagement and disagreement on this topic? Or, am I trying to convince my students to see the world my way?' Questions like this can help us to critically reflect on our practice and to recalibrate it to meet the goal of raising awareness and modelling respectful engagement better.

Finally, critical reflection allows us to ensure that we are providing our students with exposure to a fuller spectrum of locally relevant LGBTQ+ identities and perspectives. When I first started getting into LGBTQ+ work in TESOL/applied linguistics, I often felt that my work was sufficient because it moved the needle—I had created space for my students to engage with a range of lesbian and gay identities in a variety of contexts. It was not until I was giving a talk at a small, regional conference that I was forced to slow down and reflect when an attendee pointed out that in my fifteen minute talk I had not once mentioned bisexual or transgender concerns or how I brought them up with my students. It was then that I realized just how invisible and underexplored bisexual, transgender, queer, and gender non-conforming issues are in the ELT literature, and perhaps even more so in many of our classes. It was this act of being forced to slow down and critically reflect on my own practice that brought me face to face with an invisibility and marginalisation that I was inadvertently perpetuating even in my attempts to create a more inclusive educational space. So, asking ourselves questions like 'Am I representing more than just mainstream LGBTQ+ (read: gay and lesbian) lives and bodies in my work with my students?' and 'Am I inadvertently perpetuating the invisibility or stereotyping of any of the groups in my pedagogy?' are vital and ongoing steps in our efforts to queer the English language classroom.

Our Students

To continue refining our queered practice, and to ensure that we are meeting the needs of our students, we must also reflect on how our students encounter and engage with our pedagogy. A large portion of this chapter will be dedicated to tools that you can use to gauge student reactions to the queered classroom space and what to do with that feedback. Here, however, allow me to say that we must be sensitive to the myriad ways in which our students provide us with feedback. Our students provide us with feedback in both active ways, like acting out during a lesson that more centrally features LGBTQ+ themes, and in more tacit ones, like non-engagement with LGBTQ+ content and activities. In the moment, however, we may miss some of the subtler cues from our students. This means that we must take the time to critically reflect on perceived student reactions to our LGBTQ+-inclusive pedagogies by asking ourselves questions such as 'Is this student's non-engagement imagined or actual?' and 'If a student chooses not to engage with the queer classroom space, what might be driving that behaviour and how can I modify my teaching to better reach that student?' While it may be that the student is just going through a silent period (see Krashen 1985), it is also possible that what you are seeing is a negative reaction to the LGBTQ+-inclusive lessons. In which case, providing that student with a more private chance to express their feelings, such as during office hours or after class, may be an important step to showing them that you value all opinions, not just ones that conform to your worldview. Doing so allows you to reaffirm the importance of the approach that you're taking.

The Institution

We must also critically reflect on how our queered pedagogical approach interfaces and integrated with our institutional setting. This includes carefully considering its place in the curriculum (see Chapter 6) and the reactions of administrators, peers, and parental stakeholders. While I will discuss administrator, peer, and parental reactions later in this chapter, here I want to provide you with some initial questions you can ask as you begin to reflect on the interfaces between pedagogies and setting. When thinking of the curriculum, it is best to ask and occasionally revisit your answers to questions like, 'How does a queer pedagogical approach support curricular goals and outcomes?' and 'How does using a queer approach extend what students would learn otherwise, adding value to the education?'. Answering these questions, and revisiting them once a semester, can offer you invaluable insights on how to tailor your queer pedagogy to meet institutional needs better. Moreover, it can prepare you to address issues of resistance. Reflecting on the actual or potential reactions of your peers and administrators can also be a valuable exercise in ensuring a critical approach to your practice. For example, asking questions like, 'How can I help my peers/administrators better understand my approach?' or 'What questions might my administrator ask about why I'm using this approach?' can help you to both reflect on your current practice and proactively plan how you will address resistance and misunderstanding when it arises.

These are just three areas upon which you must reflect to take a critical approach to your queer practice. In the remainder of this chapter, I will discuss tools and strategies that you can use as you seek to gauge reactions and overcome resistance as you craft more LGBTQ+-inclusive English language classroom spaces, focusing first on students then on institutional considerations. Throughout this chapter, we must focus on how the feedback we receive from the various stakeholders can be used to drive our critical reflection and 'restive problematizing' of our practice (Pennycook 2001).

Gauging Responses to the Queer Classroom

Finding ways to gauge students' responses to your use of queered pedagogy is an important step in maintaining critical perspective. Since this is the stakeholder population that has direct experience with your efforts to make the classroom more LGBTQ+ inclusive, they will have valuable insights that can guide the revision of pedagogical practices and curricular materials. Note, here, that disconfirmatory voices have as many valuable insights as confirmatory ones. That is, the students that disagree with your use of a queer pedagogy can provide feedback that is just as useful as the students that love it and appreciate the representation. This is also, admittedly, one area where the TESOL and applied linguistics literature simply has not kept up. There are studies that report on *why* students take part in English language courses that specifically target members of the LGBTQ+ (Moore 2016), and that talk about students' desires for more LGBTQ+-inclusive classes (Curran 2006; Moita-Lopes 2006). There is little scholarship, however, on how students respond to the queered classroom space (see Paiz and Zhu 2018). And, there is nothing that gives voice to the students who encounter LGBTQ+-inclusive pedagogy and have a negative reaction because of pre-existing attitudes towards the LGBTQ+ community. While some may argue that this would legitimize potentially discriminatory views, I must disagree. If we only focus on the positive feedback to our attempts to queer the classroom, then we functionally hamstring ourselves as we attempt to revise our approach to reach out to more students. Also, as I have argued above, queering the English language classroom is not about winning over hearts and minds, it is about creating space for engagement with LGBTQ+ issues and modelling respectful engagement—which must necessarily account for views that fall across the spectrum of acceptance.

So, this raises a few questions:

1 What kind of data should I collect from my students?

2 How do I gauge their reactions in a way that can inform my practice?

3 What kinds of revisions to my queer pedagogy might I make based on this feedback?

Regarding the first and second questions, you should look for both informal and formal opportunities to gather information from your students about your use of a queered English language pedagogy. *Informal feedback* can come in those moments after class or during office hours when a student continues a classroom conversation. During these moments, students may share with you their feelings about a lesson by offering advice in both direct ('I wish we could spend more time talking about the different kinds of family') and indirect ways ('My friend is in Ms Zhang's class and they didn't talk about this topic in the same way we did'). You may also get informal feedback during class lessons by watching the underlife and students' embodied reactions while you teach (Brooke 1987). For example, two students may begin chatting quietly about something seemingly off-topic instead of engaging with the material, or you may notice closed-off body language (e.g. crossed arms, lack of eye contact, etc.). Be watching out for signs of underlife or negative reactions and where they are happening in the lesson, as they may signal discomfort with the material. This awareness can then be used as a starting point for you to critically reflect on how you might better prepare students for the LGBTQ+-inclusive lessons and content that they will encounter in your class.

Formal feedback, on the other hand, is purpose-built to gather more actionable data to drive your reflections on and revision of your queered practice. At present, there are no pre-made tools to help gauge students' reactions to LGBTQ+ content. However, this should not detract you from gathering formal feedback throughout the process of deploying your queer inquiry-informed pedagogy. For example, you may want to consider using a modified version of a survey like the attitudes survey that I have described elsewhere in a conversation on negotiating LGBTQ+ inclusion (Paiz 2020b). This survey can be used to provide you with a quick reading of students' current awareness of LGBTQ+ issues and their initial comfort levels with discussing them as part of the class (see Figure 5.1). The goal of this survey is not to decide whether to include LGBTQ+ themes but to inform where you decide to start the conversation. It may uncover that there is a need to talk about why LGBTQ+ issues matter, even in the English language class, before deploying inclusive materials and lessons.

Additionally, you might consider through a web-based survey using Qualtrics or Google Forms after using an LGBTQ+-themed lesson to both gauge student learning and their reactions to the lesson. Here, asking modified forms of the questions in Alber (2013) can provide useful fuel for your critical reflections:

- What do you think about the inclusive lesson that we just had?
- Why do you think that?
- How did you come to think that?

- Can you tell me more?
- What questions do you still have?

These questions seek to gauge students' initial emotional reaction to a lesson, what they feel they have learned, and what is still a source of possible confusion or misunderstanding. These questions take an open-ended format and can be completed in about 10 to 15 minutes.

Based on student feedback and in-class reactions, you may find the need to adjust either your materials, your pedagogical approach, or both.

1. I have friends who are members of or have a connection to (e.g., a family member or close friend), the LGBTQ+ community.
   a. Yes
   b. No
   c. Don't know
   d. Prefer not to answer
2. LGBTQ+ issues are not talked about enough in our class' activities and materials.
   a. Agree
   b. Disagree
   c. Unsure
   d. Prefer not to answer
3. LGBTQ+ issues affect straight students and LGBTQ+ ones.
   a. Agree
   b. Disagree
   c. Unsure
   d. Prefer not to answer
4. LGBTQ+ issues are important today.
   a. Agree
   b. Disagree
   c. Unsure
   d. Prefer not to answer
5. I feel comfortable talking about LGBTQ+ topics in class.
   a. Agree
   b. Disagree
   c. Unsure
   d. Prefer not to answer
6. I feel comfortable talking about LGBTQ+ topics in private.
   a. Agree
   b. Disagree
   c. Unsure
   d. Prefer not to answer

Figure 5.1 Example 'Opening Attitudes Survey'.

Source: based on Paiz (2020b)

This act of revision is an essential part of maintaining a critical approach to your queer pedagogy. Yes, it may add to the work that you must do, but it will help you refine your LGBTQ+ pedagogy to be maximally beneficial to your students and your institutional context. Based on what has been reported on in the literature, and my experiences using queer inquiry-based pedagogies in my own practice, here are three common types of revisions that you may find yourself making based upon feedback from your students.

The first revision that you may need to make is in how you scaffold your efforts to include more LGBTQ+ content and themes in your classroom instruction. Curran (2006), for example, reports on a less-than-successful lesson on Sydney Gay and Lesbian Mardi Gras, an annual event that mirrors Pride in many other national contexts. In his lesson, he began from the assumption that as a gay man who has participated in Mardi Gras he would be well positioned to teach his ESL students about this event in the context of local holiday celebrations. What he found, however, was that what he had assumed as a linguistic and cultural starting point was a bit ahead of where the students where, as evidenced by poor performance on comprehension questions and repeated requests to explain specific lexical and cultural tokens in greater detail. Moments like this, where we overestimate our students' awareness of LGBTQ+ conversations underscore how we might need to build additional scaffolds into our lessons. In Curran's (2006) case, this meant revising the lesson to include pre-study material introducing some language that was specific to the local LGBTQ+ community. You may find the need to include this kind of explicit language support in your own lessons. For example, you may have students read a text like *I am Jazz* (Herthel and Jennings 2014), an illustrated story that discusses transgender experiences, and you may find that there are issues understanding terms like 'transgender', 'gender identity', or 'gender-expression'. In this case, you may want to consider a 'Transgender-inclusive Language List' based on resources like those from the National Center for Transgender Equality (NCTE 2016) or the University of Maryland's Lesbian, Gay, Bisexual and Transgender Equity Center (UMD Equity Center n.d.). Building in additional linguistic scaffolding like this can be helpful to students who are both new to engaging with LGBTQ+ content and are new to the language used to do so.

A second frequent revision is focused on the specific materials you end up deploying. You may choose to have students in an EAP or IEP academic literacy course read something like the executive summary to Human Rights Watch's (2016) report on the challenges LGBT students in US schools with the hope of exposing students to LGBTQ+ content and authentic academic/professional writing. However, given the nature of the report, you may find that students are not responding to the material in the way that you hoped. This is a case where swapping out this resource for a more locally relevant one, such as student rights and engagement resources from a local university's LGBTQ+ centre (e.g. LGBTQ Center at UNC n.d.), may prove more effective. The students may respond better to the local resource because the information will resonate more with their lived experiences, showing that LGBTQ+ issues matter to the institution and also modelling the local community's use of respectful language and engagement. Moreover, students may be more interested in materials that speak more directly to their lived experiences than one that they see as more distant because they speak to more nebulous 'national concerns' of a country that may not be their home country, as is the case for international and study away students.

The third most common revision has to do with time commitments. You may be tempted to try to shoehorn LGBTQ+-inclusive lessons into single 50- or 75-minute blocks throughout your curriculum. However, these discussions often require more time to unpack for students and to work through with them as they come to master the language, content, and communicative strategies to respectfully engage with LGBTQ+ discussions and individuals (see Merse 2017). Be prepared to revise your lesson plans to include space for students' engagement with LGBTQ+-inclusive ideas to develop. This may mean building in cool-down time if in-class passions for the topic (both positive and negative) begin to flare; or, it may mean adding in time at the beginning of the next class period for students to bring up additional questions or concerns.

Navigating Challenges

You will, without a doubt, face challenges as you seek to deploy a queer inquiry-based pedagogy in your English language classes. While finding materials and preparing lessons are one form of challenge, here, we will focus on the resistance that you may face from various stakeholder populations. Resistance can take many forms; but no matter the shape, it works against your attempts to make the classroom a more critical and inclusive space. Note, however, that facing resistance from students, peers, administrators, and parents is different from working in a *frigid context* (see Paiz 2020a; Pawelczyk, Pakuła, and Sunderland 2014). Frigid contexts are those settings where either institutional or legal pressures exist that would cause a teacher using a queered pedagogy to face penalties that may include the loss of their job or personal freedoms (for an extended discussion, see the Afterward). This, section will focus on the three central stakeholder populations from whom you may face varying levels of resistance: students, administrators, and parents. After outlining some of the forms of resistance you may face from these groups, I will discuss how you can use these experiences to help you maintain criticality in your use of LGBTQ+-inclusive pedagogies.

Student Resistance

We spend the bulk of our professional lives with our students. They are also the ones with the greatest exposure and potential to inform our queered pedagogical approaches. Simply put, students are our most significant stakeholder population—more important, I would argue, than any other because all that we do should, ideally, be in service to their needs. If you are reading this book, if you are interested in making your classroom more inclusive of marginalized groups, then you are doing so because you feel it will significantly benefit this population. You will likely face both active and passive resistance from different groups of students as you deploy and refine your queered pedagogy.

Active resistance can be somewhat jarring as it takes the form of students vocally pushing back against your instructional efforts (see Nicol 2006). For example, you may decide to use an illustrated narrative activity, like the one discussed in Chapter 4, where students read a story featuring LGBTQ+ themes and engage with the linguistic and rhetorical ways in which LGBTQ+-identities and experiences are indexed. One form of active resistance that you may face is for a student to, sometimes rather vocally and passionately, tell you that they find this kind of activity wildly inappropriate because it deals with a 'deviant' or 'sinful' group of people. The student may even use forcefully homophobic language in registering their feelings with you. At that moment, it can be easy to react, to shut down the conversation, to pull rank on the student. This is a dangerous move because it signals to all students that force must be met with force and that non-engagement is a good communicative and argumentative strategy when encountering people whose worldview radically differs from one's own. Yes, abusive language should not be tolerated in the classroom. Disengaging from tough conversations, however, is not the right behaviour to model.

Instead, when you face this form of active resistance, use it as a chance to model respectful engagement and useful linguistic structures for disagreeing and social justice advocacy for your students. If passions flair too much, if the resistance is too high, certainly tell students that you are going to pause the day's activities. Be explicit with why you are doing so. For example, if homophobic or transphobic language is being used, identify it as such and be specific about what makes it homophobic or transphobic. Tell them why and how it goes against the spirit of respectful engagement that is a vital part of your course. Acknowledge the dissenting student's right to disagree with the material and their potentially strong feelings about it. Then, set a date for when the class will revisit the conversation after tempers have cooled down. Once you do so, it may be useful to discuss how to disagree more respectfully and strategies to make a dissenting opinion known while still be respectful of others.

Passive resistance is a bit tougher both to identify and address. In a class of 20 to 50 students, it can be difficult to gauge every students' reaction, to catch every furrowed brow or crossed set of arms. When students passively resist queer pedagogical approaches, they will disengage from the lesson in less disruptive ways—checking their mobiles, skipping class meetings, or sitting silently in the back. This form of resistance must still be acknowledged and addressed, but it may be best to do so through one-to-one engagement with the student or group of students, as opposed to with the whole class. When you face passive resistance in the classroom, set up the task for the engaged students and once they are working and you have addressed initial questions, approach the disengaged student and use the strategies you would typically use—ask about the student's well-being and express your concern over their non-engagement. If they say that they do not like talking about LGBTQ+ issues, remind them that part of your class, and learning English to advanced proficiency, is being able to talk through culturally sensitive issues in ways that do not threaten interpersonal relationships. Again, acknowledge their right to disagree and hear them out. This is where individualized instruction might help show that you value their contributions, even if they are divergent from your personal views. Work with them to find ways to express their opinions with the class respectfully. If they continue to pushback, ask them to work on an alternative project where they reflect on why they are disengaging from the lesson and why they find this kind of curricular content so challenging. This requires them to still engage with LGBTQ+ issues, but it gives them a more private platform to express themselves. You can then provide the student with feedback through formative commentary on the alternative assignment.

Passive resistance often presents us with the greatest chance to critically reflect on our pedagogy and to make changes that will be helpful to all of our students. For example, you may find the need to build in additional scaffolding before you use of LGBTQ+-inclusive materials or activities that engage more directly with LGBTQ+ concerns. Alternatively, you might find the need to revise your course syllabus with a 'respect and professionalism' statement to more explicitly remind students of what to do when they encounter potentially contentious course themes. Finally, it may lay bare the opportunity for alternative methods of allowing students to engage with the queer classroom space through individualized instructions and alternative assignments. What is important in all these cases is that you are not providing the students with a proverbial way out, rather you are providing them with a more private initial platform to engage. Proactive planning is the best strategy for overcoming student resistance. As you are crafting your LGBTQ+-inclusive pedagogy, consider the points at which you feel you are most likely to encounter resistance and have a few alternative strategies queued up.

Administrator Resistance

It is not uncommon to face administrative resistance over the use of queer inquiry-based pedagogies. Administrators' concerns range from worries that including LGBTQ+ content and themes will alienate key client populations, to concerns that they will detract from other educational goals and outcomes or will anger parents or accreditors. Facing administrative resistance can be daunting because of the potential power dynamic that may exist between teaching faculty and administrators and because many English language specialists find themselves in contingent or support roles, especially in American educational contexts, creating a genuine concern over continued employment (see also Curran 2006; Ó'Móchain 2006; Pawelczyk, Pakuła, and Sunderland 2014). Administrative resistance can be challenging to work through, but there are options for how to frame the conversation, assuming your administrator is willing to discuss the matter.

One useful strategy is to tie your use of an LGBTQ+-inclusive curriculum to broader programmatic or institutional goals such as inculcating critical thinking skills, fostering acculturation, or providing an authentic approach to language teaching and learning. Wherever possible, use the language of the institution, as reflected in values and mission statements to help you build your case for the use of queered pedagogies in ELT. Being prepared with examples of how your queer pedagogy serves as an educational means for course goals to become measurable course outcomes is also a useful strategy to overcoming resistance. For example, if one of the goals for your course is for students to be able to use English to debate important topics in academic settings, you can show how using a queer inquiry-based pedagogy requires students to be critical about information and their own beliefs as they make sense of the world. You can then show how this is reflected in student work through the research they do in building their positions. Alternatively, you could invite your administrator to observe one of the classes where you are directly engaging with LGBTQ+ content or themes. Often, administrative resistance comes from a well-intentioned but misguided place, one of misunderstand and fear. So, inviting them into your classroom space to show the value of your pedagogical approach can be a powerful tool. Granted, some administrators may choose to lead through fiat. In this case, having the buy-in of a well-connected and more established peer may be helpful.

When you encounter administrative resistance, you will still find kernels of ideas that you can use to drive your critical reflection on your queered practice. For example, if the administrator expresses concerns about LGBTQ+-inclusive content taking away from 'more important' material that students need for standardized tests, you can begin considering how your approach supplements the traditional materials and may lead to the same educational. Alternatively, you may decide to revise your syllabus or your teaching philosophy to directly highlight how your queer inquiry-based pedagogy directly addresses the goals, means, and outcomes of your course in the wider institutional context.

Parental Resistance

Perhaps more common in K-12 settings, it is also common to face parental resistance. This kind of resistance can be particularly vocal and even garner national attention (e.g. Boroff 2018; Eyewitness News 2018; Pulver 2015). Parents may object to what they see as your attempts to 'indoctrinate' their child; or, they may protest on religious grounds. In any of these cases, begin by listening and acknowledging the parents right to voice their views. If they are willing to listen and to engage with you, as opposed to react, share with them your teaching philosophy and why you feel it is important to take an inclusive approach to language education, drawing connections to the negative effects faced by other marginalized populations. If, however, the resistance is particularly fierce you may want to enlist the help of a sympathetic administrator to guide the conversation. And, if the parents threaten to have you removed because of your 'obscene influence', be prepared by connecting with groups like Lambda Legal in the US, or the Law Society's LGBT+ Lawyers Division in the UK to help safeguard your rights. While it would be ideal to work with parents to highlight the value of a queer inquiry-based approach to language teaching, this may not always be possible because of ossified, homophobic/transphobic beliefs.

Facing parental resistance may also provide you with important insights to drive your critical reflection. For example, based on parental conversations, you may choose to update (or create) your 'about me' information that you share with parents and students at the beginning of the term. In it, you might discuss your use of queer inquiry-based approaches and what you see them adding to the classroom and student's education. You might also decide to create a sort of FAQ for your professional website where you address common questions that parents have about LGBTQ+-inclusive classrooms—its scope, the kinds of content students encounter, and your respect for students with opinions that differ from your own.

Conclusion

Maintaining a critical stance towards your queer pedagogy is essential in keeping with the spirit of critical approaches to ELT and the core of queer inquiry-based pedagogies (Nelson 2009; Pennycook 2001; Chapter 2, this volume). Therefore, you must be prepared to engage in 'restive problematizing' of your practice. Proactively working to gauge how your students respond to your use of LGBTQ+-inclusive materials and classroom practices is a crucial aspect of maintaining a critical view, as it allows you to gather input from your most important stakeholders and tailor your efforts to meet their educational and acculturational needs. Navigating resistance to your use of queered approaches to ELT is another vital facet of remaining critical, as it can provide you with surprising insights that will make your practice more effective. This chapter provided you with actionable recommendations for making both of these—gauging reactions and navigating challenges—part of your queer toolkit.

Key Takeaways

Engaging in the seemingly ceaseless problematizing of our practice can be an intimidating prospect, in no small part because it seems to feed into the problematic discourse of endless improvement. However, it is an important act to ensure that we are providing a thorough and equitable view of LGBTQ+ considerations to our students. Moreover, it is vital to ensuring that our own biases and assumptions about LGBTQ+ lives, our students, and their needs do not override actual need on the part of our stakeholder. Common critiques of critical approaches are that nothing is ever good enough; they do not celebrate successes, and trouble everything to the point of inaction (see Pennycook 2001). However, engaging in the kind of restive problematizing called for in this chapter is geared towards honing your LGBTQ+-inclusive practice in context-specific ways so that it can better give voice, and perhaps even hope, to marginalized groups in your English language classroom and equip your students to be more active global citizens.

Resistance to queer-inclusive course design is to be expected and can come in a myriad of shapes and degrees. Student resistance, for example, can take both *active* and *passive* forms. It is important to be mindful of both types of resistance in your classroom and to use proactive planning to help mitigate its effects. You might begin by providing students with ample opportunities to provide you with *in situ* and post-class feedback that you can then use to revise your approach. To goal is not to remove or tone down the LGBTQ+-inclusive content, but to better prepare students for it and to more ethically make space for dissenting voices. Resistance from peers, administrators, and parents is also a possibility and can be a particularly frightening one. However, having well-positioned allies, thought out responses, and clear connections between your efforts to queer the English language classroom and course or programmatic goals and outcomes can all help you navigate the proverbial chop that you might encounter. Moreover, these moments of resistance provide you with more fodder for your critical reflection that can drive impactful revise to your practice.

Reflective Praxis Prompt

To help you consider how the ideas of this chapter might integrate with your own practice, consider the following questions:

- How do I think my students will react when I deploy a more explicitly LGBTQ+-inclusive lesson?
- What worries me about the possible negative reactions that I might face from students, peers, administrators, and parents?
- What allies might I be able to call on to help me navigate these challenges?
- What proactive plans can I make to account for these challenges?
- How will I communicate the value of an LGBTQ+-inclusive English language pedagogy to others?

6

Goals and Outcomes of the Queered Classroom

Introduction

Previous chapters have positioned queer inquiry-based pedagogies into the broader constellation of TESOL and applied linguistics research and scholarship and have provided you with the strategies and tools that you can use adapt it in ways that are locally situated and responsive to students' needs and lived experiences. This chapter focuses on how to tie your queered pedagogy to course and institutional learning goals and outcomes. Taking the time to articulate how your queered approach speaks to learning goals and outcomes provides an opportunity to speak to the relevance of using such an approach, which can then be used to facilitate discussions with relevant stakeholders.

This chapter will also provide you with the necessary tools-for-thought to begin developing locally relevant goals for your LGBTQ+-inclusive courses and lessons. Making the learning goals locally relevant allows you to meet students where they are at when it comes to their engagement with critical approaches and the inclusion of LGBTQ+ content and materials. Additionally, it allows you to begin connecting course discussions on LGBTQ+ issues to the students' daily lives, underscoring for them the fact that LGBTQ+ matters are not distant problems that can be ignored. Rather, they are part of their local communities and daily lives, even if they have been rendered invisible and salient by local discourses.

General Goals and Outcomes of the Queered Classroom Space

It is important to devise tailored goals that are aligned to the needs of your local context. However, there are a few goals and their related outcomes that are likely to be germane across contexts. These goals and outcomes, to which your queered pedagogy is the means, form a starting point for finding linkages to course and institutional goals. The common goals for queer inquiry-based pedagogies are (1) raising awareness, (2) valuing sexual diversity, and (3) facilitating dialogue.

Goal 1: Awareness Raising and Establishing Relevance

The first classroom goal of any queer inquiry-based pedagogy is to raise students' awareness of LGBTQ+ lives and issues and how they may present in their local context, whether it is a temporary one (such as a study away site), or a more permanent one (such as their hometown). Because our students do not represent a monolithic population, instead coming to us from disparate sociocultural backgrounds, they bring with them varying degrees of exposure to and comfort with LGBTQ+ content and issues. So, getting LGBTQ+ issues on our students' collective radar is an essential starting point and a manageable first goal.

The advice provided in Chapter 3 represents some of the methods available to you to help raise student awareness. In your deployment of a queer inquiry-based pedagogy, you may also find it necessary to work towards establishing the relevance of LGBTQ+ issues to your students' language learning and acculturational needs. The latter is especially relevant in the case of students who are studying, or desiring to study, in places such as the United States, the United Kingdom, Canada, New Zealand, etc. In seeking to establish the relevance of the topic, it is often important to consider how you will first bring LGBTQ+ content and themes into your classroom and how you will meet your students where they are at. For example, Güney (2019) reported on her use of a Turkish documentary that discussed the life of a transgender person from a small town in Turkey to make the topic's relevance more immediately salient to her students and to begin breaking down resistance to a queered classroom approach. By using a local example, she was able to show her students that what some may have considered a predominately 'Western' issue was in all actuality much more immediate.

Goal 2: Valuing Sexual Diversity

Showing students why sexual diversity should be valued is another important classroom goal for your queer inquiry-based pedagogy. By deploying the strategies and content called for in Chapters 3 and 4, you begin showing your student that both you personally, and many contexts that use the target language, value sexual diversity as a legitimate part of human experiences and individual's lives. In creating value around sexual diversity, use your pedagogical approach to address ways that sexual diversity adds to and enhances society. For example, you may choose to supplement a lesson on the family by looking at LGBTQ+ families that have adopted their children, drawing attention to how LGBTQ+ adoption often provides a loving, stable, lifelong home to a child that might otherwise be a ward of the state. By adopting, LGBTQ+ parents not only make a decision that benefits the child, but that also provide more extensive social benefits like increased average lifetime income of adopted children and decreased government spending (see Eschelbach Hansen 2006).

Goal 3: Facilitating Dialogue

Getting students talking about issues of sexuality, gender, and social justice is both a general and an educational goal of queer inquiry-based pedagogies. Facilitated dialogue between students on critical issues can be helpful in both destigmatizing certain topics of conversation and in coming to understand communicative strategies better—both locally and interculturally. For example, during a discussion of a short story that includes LGBTQ+ themes or issues, students may naturally take differing positions about how the story presented LGBTQ+ lives in broader social contexts, how the story interfaces with their own thoughts and understandings, or how the views of the story (dis-)align with how these issues are (not) discussed in their home contexts. By allowing space for all voices a queer inquiry-based pedagogy, with the guidance of the educator, can lead to a dialogue where all students feel heard. Moreover, by having a focal text, students learn to negotiate meaning through dialogue and can be exposed to useful local strategies to repair misunderstandings. At a more global level, facilitating dialogue, and making space for diverse voices, can facilitate the acquisition of intercultural competence because it gives students real-world experience navigating sensitive topics with peers that come from different big- or small-c cultural orientations.

Related to these three classroom goals, there are also three general outcomes that represent the habits of mind, understandings, and linguistic/rhetorical skills that our students should possess or be progressing towards after they leave queered classroom spaces. The outcomes presented here are only general starting points. You will need to tailor additional learning outcomes based on your local context, which I will discuss later in this chapter. Also, bear in mind that these outcomes represent ideal endpoints, and are not, therefore, mandated targets. In many cases, making progress towards these outcomes represents essential steps forward as we work to meet our students where they are at in regards to their engagement with LGBTQ+ considerations.

Outcome 1: A Better Understanding of LGBTQ+ Issues.

The chief educational outcome of an LGBTQ+ inclusive pedagogy is that students will have a better understanding of LGBTQ+ issues and lives. This goal is in direct response to Krause's (2017) admonition that queer approaches to TESOL must not view their end goal as an evangelical one of hearts and minds, but instead of moving the needle on students' understandings. That is, your deployment of a queer inquiry-based pedagogy does not seek the radical transformation of personal beliefs and attitudes—although for some this may happen from time to time. Rather, it seeks a gradual change through awareness raising and exposure to authentic LGBTQ+ lives, bodies, texts, and experiences. For example, you can use a slightly modified version of the attitudes survey discussed in Chapter 5 as a form of an exit survey. You can then compare class- or course-level responses to uncover positive or negative changes in attitudes towards LGBQ+ issues, which you can use to gauge progress and to fuel revisions of your queered approach. When measuring this outcome, it is vital to focus on class- or course-levels and to not focus on individual learners, as this would not respect the different starting points and pathways of the learners.

Outcome 2: Critical Habits of Mind

Another outcome of the queered classroom space is for students to exhibit critical habits of mind when it comes to language, social issues, and knowledge. Being able to exhibit critical thinking is often a vital learning outcome of many classes—especially in writing, EAP, and IEP courses located in traditionally defined ESL contexts. Throughout the courses where you are deploying a queered pedagogy, you will want to make space for formative and summative assessments of students' progress towards acquiring more critical habits of mind. There are many ways to do this that are often already part of your classroom practice, such as requiring students to include dissenting voices in argumentative essays, completing source analysis assignments (e.g. the CRAAP test), or having them show an awareness of other perspectives when they discuss their topics with you after class or during office hours.

Outcome 3: Linguistic and Rhetorical Skills for Respectful Engagement

Finally, gaining the linguistic and rhetorical skills necessary to participate in respectful engagement with LGBTQ+ topics and individuals is a key learning outcome of any queer-inclusive pedagogy. It is important because of how central it is both to helping students to become participants in non-marginalizing discourses about sexual minorities, but also because working towards this outcome equips students with the skills that they need to perform locally relevant identities and to advocate for themselves and others. Measuring progress towards this outcome may feel like it is the easiest of the three. For example, you may compare how students engage with and talk or write about LGBTQ+ topics in assignments at earlier and later points in the semester, noting changes in the argumentative approach, types of evidence that they use to support their claims, or the use of more respectful terms (e.g. transgender person vs. transvestite, etc.). Note that what is important here is whether or not the students show evidence of progress in using respectful language and rhetorical strategies, not that they necessarily agree with your personal views on the matters. Remember, exposure and awareness raising; not hearts and minds.

The goals and outcomes presented above are the general goals and educational outcomes for any queer inclusive pedagogy in ELT. It will be up to you to use these starting points to develop goals and objectives that speak to your unique contextual demands. Your reflections on your use of a queer inquiry-based pedagogy, conversations with peers and administrators, and your knowledge of your local context will drive much of your localization efforts. The rest of this chapter will offer you tools-for-thought on how to begin this essential work. Additionally, recall that pre-planning activities such as creating clearly articulated, locally relevant learning goals and outcomes can be critical in overcoming any resistant that you might face to deploying your queer inquiry-based pedagogy.

Fitting Queer Goals into Pre-existing Institutional Spaces

One of the challenges that we often face in deploying LGBTQ+-inclusive pedagogies is making them knowable to our colleagues, students, administrators, and parental stakeholders. This challenge can increase the resistance that we face in deploy these pedagogies, as others may have false presuppositions about what queered pedagogy's goals are and what it looks like in classroom practice. By fitting our queer inquiry-based pedagogies' goals and outcomes into pre-existing institutional spaces, we can render them more knowable to the various stakeholders in our disciplinary contexts. This act of linking is best done by finding room in either institutional goal and mission statements, or in class-specific goals, means, and outcomes statements.

In the pre-K-12 context, your institution may be using goals and outcomes that strive to meet requirements from larger regulatory bodies. In some cases, these may be related to guidance from international professional organizations like TESOL International Association. For example, TESOL International Association (2006) outlines the development of communicative competence in the areas of language arts, mathematics, and the sciences as central goals that school-based ESL programmes should meet to be compliant with No Child Left Behind and Common Core standards in the US. They also advocate for helping students gain increased intercultural competence to facilitate both interpersonal and classroom conversations.

Using these standards as a starting point, you can link the use of a queer-inclusive pedagogy to institutional goals in many ways. For example in many Western contexts, it may be easy to argue that conversations about sexuality and sexual identity are central parts of students' lived experiences, especially at more advanced grades, and that an LGBTQ+-inclusive ESL curriculum facilitates this transition from both linguistic and acculturational perspectives (see also Alexander 2008; Moita-Lopes 2006). For younger grade levels, making connections to helping students integrate with the diverse student body at the school, which may include transgender children or parents who are members of the LGBTQ+ community, can also be a productive way of connecting your queer inquiry-based pedagogy back to the local institutional context.

In IEP and EAP settings, many institutions have the goal of preparing students for university-level study or work in inter-/transnational contexts. In these cases, situating the goals and outcomes of your queered pedagogy into those of the larger institution is a relatively easy task. Making these linkages apparent is made easier by the fact that you can show how a critical, queer approach prepares students for the kinds of critical thinking tasks they will need to complete in their university courses post-matriculation or will prepare them to respectfully engage with sexually diverse colleagues when they enter the workforce. Even in the context of more liberal religious institutions, there is the possibility to make a case for your queer pedagogy by linking it very clearly to programmatic goals and outcomes through the use of locally relevant materials (Güney 2019; Ó'Móchain 2006).

In programmes situated in the traditionally defined EFL context, it may be more challenging to make clear connections between the goals of queer inquiry-based pedagogy and broader institutional mission. However, it is still possible by digging into the language of the institution's mission and vision statements. Take the mission of New Oriental Education and Technology Group, which is one of the premier English language teaching outfits in China, as one example. Its website states that their goal is to equip students with the language that they need to 'achieve a brighter future' (New Oriental n.d.). Even this nebulous language provides a pathway to situating your use of queer inquiry-based pedagogies. For example, you can begin by acknowledging that, especially in urban China, professional knowledge workers often interface with international and transnational workplaces. And, in such liminal spaces, we must often engage with diverse ideas, peoples, and beliefs. Since one goal of a queered pedagogy is to equip students for respectful engagement with culturally sensitive conversations, the approach is directly in-line with the goal of helping students achieve better futures through language because they will be more adequately prepared to work with colleagues that come from diverse backgrounds in ways that facilitate mutual respect and understanding.

Developing Locally Relevant Goals

Beyond situating your queered pedagogy into broader institutional discourses, you should also plan on developing locally relevant goals and outcomes. While making connections to the institution can help make the importance of your approach more salient to your peers and administrators, crafting goals specific to your classroom or group of learners can help you to make your approach more accessible and understandable to your students. You may choose to tailor language, intercultural communication/understanding, and habits-of-mind goals to your classroom.

For example, in a middle school sheltered ESL course that focuses on language acquisition and acculturation, you may choose to craft a specific linguistic goal for students as they encounter your queered classroom space. Perhaps, you want them to expand their understanding of proper pronoun usage to include an understanding of singular 'they/their' along with the interpersonal competence to navigate how personal pronouns play an essential role in respectfully engaging with trans and gender non-conforming individuals. Alternatively, you may want them to expand their linguistic understanding of family to include gender-neutral terms in discussing familial relations (e.g. spouse/partner vs husband/wife). Whatever local goals you chose to include for you queered pedagogy, it is essential that they meet the needs of the group of learners with whom you are working. If, for example, you work in a school with a robust gay–straight alliance, or where students are more keyed into issues of diversity, equity, and inclusion, then these goals may be too simplistic. You may need to revise them to move the needle further for how students come to make sense of and engage with issues of sexual diversity in their L2s.

In an adult education setting, on the other hand, you may choose to develop localized goals that speak more to increasing intercultural awareness and communicative competence. These goals may focus more on raising students' general awareness of LGBTQ+ issues in the local community, and at the institution. Alternatively, they may focus on students exhibiting, whether they are ideologically opposed to LGBTQ+ lives or not, that they understand why being able to talk about these issues in a measured, non-discriminatory way is important in local educational and workplace settings. Meanwhile, in a four-year college or university setting, you may set goals where students show that hold certain habits of the mind that are closely tied to the more general goals and outcomes of a queer inquiry-based pedagogy. For example, if you are in a programme that has sheltered L2 composition courses, after which students will be mainstreamed, you may create goals related to critical information literacy and more objective argumentation from sources, as these may be skills they will need in their disciplinary courses or later in core curriculum classes.

While the examples above may infer a move from concrete to more abstract goals based upon the grade level of your students, you should choose classroom goals that fit your learners, their needs, and your hopes for what skills, habits, and knowledge they will possess when they leave your class. It is entirely possible to create goals focused on critical thinking and source engagement in K-12 settings, and equally likely that you will have foundational linguistic goals for adult education and EAP/IEP courses. What matters most is that your decisions about what goals to set and how to sequence them in your course are based on your understanding of your learners and their educational needs and that they are in service to their future linguistic, rhetorical, and acculturational needs.

Conclusion

Articulating the goals and learning outcomes for your queered pedagogy is an essential move in rendering your efforts to queer the English language classroom knowable and understandable to the various stakeholders—students, parents, peers, and administrators—that may encounter it. Moreover, tying these goals and outcomes to broader institutional ones can help overcome resistance to your queered pedagogy and emphasize the appropriateness of queer-inclusive approaches to your programme, department, or school. More importantly, tailoring the goals to your specific class or group of students is an excellent way to both show the value of LGBTQ+-inclusive spaces and to individualize instruction to a group of students' unique needs. This chapter has sought to provide you with certain tools-for-thought to begin the work of devising these goals. In closing, I would encourage you to revisit these goals and outcomes from time-to-time just as you would any other component of your queer inquiry-based pedagogy to ensure that they still fit with your teaching philosophy and your students' educational and acculturational needs.

Key Takeaways

For this chapter, there are three main takeaways for you to bear in mind as you move through fleshing out and deploying your own queer inquiry-based pedagogy (see also Table 6.1). They are:

- Articulating clear goals and outcomes are critical to the success of your queered classroom space because they help demystify the approach for others and to make its potential value clearer.
- Taking the time to draw connections between your goals and outcomes and broader programmatic/institutional ones can help overcome resistance and create alignments between your approach and those of your programme, department, or school.
- Developing personalized goals and outcomes is an essential step in crafting your own queer inquiry-based pedagogy. While they may be based on the general ones presented in this chapter, they should speak to the needs of your group of learners.

Table 6.1 Goals and outcomes of a queer inquiry informed pedagogy.

Goals	Outcomes
Awareness raising and establishing relevance	A better understanding of local LGBTQ+ issues and their socially situated importance
Understanding and valuing sexual and gender diversity	The instillation of critical habits of mind and perspective on various ways of life
Facilitating dialogue	The acquisition of linguistic and rhetorical skills for respectful engagement with a variety of interlocutors

Reflexive Practice Prompt

Below are some questions to help guide your thinking as you consider how this chapter might interface with your own practice:

- What changes in linguistic/rhetorical abilities or understanding do I want my students to have once they leave my queered classroom space?
- What habits of mind do I want them to exhibit in their work?
- What do I hope that my students get from engaging with an LGBTQ+-inclusive classroom?
- How will I measure progress towards the goals and outcomes that I establish for my classes?

7

Conclusion

AT A GLANCE

Introduction

This book has worked to provide practitioners with an introduction to making their classrooms more LGBTQ+ inclusive by providing actionable recommendations for the adoption and adaptation of a pedagogy based on Nelson's (2006, 2009) queer inquiry. Being based on research from Queer TESOL and Lavender ALx, the recommendations in this book can speak to students' lived experiences and can be linked to emerging best practices in the fields that most closely inform ELT. Moreover, the proposed pedagogy outlined in this book can, in keeping with advances in critical ELT and ALx, speak to the need to prepare our students to be aware of the seas of privilege and oppression upon which they are themselves making a way in the world. By raising students' awareness of critical issues, and equipping them with the tools they will need to render these issues knowable and to interrogate them, we can work towards helping our students become more socially conscious global citizens.

Throughout this book, you have been introduced to rise of LGBTQ+ issues in the fields of TESOL and Applied Linguistics and the implications of this shift for ELT pedagogy. Chapter one introduced you to the notion of *queering*, or troubling, a heteronormative worldview that marginalizes sexual minorities either explicitly through oppression or implicitly through silence and invisibility. Chapter two provided you with the basics of one queer inquiry-based pedagogy and gave examples from my practice as a queer scholar that has taught in both traditionally defined ESL and EFL contexts. Chapter three shifted the conversation to providing examples of normative classroom spaces and how you could use a personally tailored queer inquiry-based pedagogy to begin troubling these spaces, making them more inclusive of all identities. Chapter four, meanwhile, cast a light upon the role of curricular materials in a queered pedagogical approach and how we can work to make even non-heteronormative texts queerer. Chapter five introduced you to the importance of pausing, reflecting, and taking the pulse of the various stakeholders with whom you work after you begin deploying your queer inquiry-based pedagogy. This gauging of reactions is vital to ensure that you are meeting on-the-ground needs and that you are engaging with students and others at a knowable and accessible place in regards to LGBTQ+ issues and content. Finally, chapter six discussed the goals of the queered classroom space and provided you with guidance on how to develop locally relevant ones. My hope, as the author, is that after reading this book you will feel more prepared to craft and use a personalized queer inquiry-based pedagogy in at least part of your teaching. Even if you roll the pedagogy out slowly, trying it on to see how it fits, I believe that you will be making a massive difference for your students. I also hope that you will feel more prepared to give queering your classroom a try, as a common complaint amongst educators is that they feel wildly underprepared to do so (see MacDonald, El Metoui, Baynham, and Gray 2014; Merse 2015; Paiz 2019). I hold this hope—both that you will try enacting what you have learned through reading this book, and that you have found it helpful—because making your classroom more LGBTQ+-inclusive matters.

The Importance of Queering the Classroom

While I acknowledge and respect the ideological diversity that exists when it comes to LGBTQ+ issues across the globe (see the Afterword), I will always firmly believe that we must work to make our classrooms more inclusive for sexual minorities. This belief is steeled by the fact that our classroom space may be the only one where LGBTQ+-identified students feel visible, where they feel heard, and where they feel safe to exist. Being seen, heard, and safe are not only crucial for human development, it is also important for language acquisition. Being seen, heard, and safe allow for the development of voice, agency over learning, and the lowering of affective barriers—all of which have been shown to facilitate SLA processes.

That being said, there are those that would disagree, or at least would voice serious concern, with the proposition in this book. In 2019, I was on a conference marathon—presenting my work on queer inclusive ELT at the meetings of the American Association for Applied Linguistics (AAAL) and the Conference on College Composition and Communication. During this trip, I also made a pit stop at TESOL to take meetings with editorial boards and to reconnect with colleagues that I only ever see at big events like this. At TESOL, I was fortunate enough to sit in on a panel presentation discussing the challenges faced by women of colour in higher education (Grant et al. 2019). What was striking during this panel was that lesbian, cis-gender women's issues were mentioned, but the challenges of being a trans woman and an ELT researcher/practitioner were never once broached by the six presenters on the panel. During a spirited discussion afterwards, Ryuko Kubota, the doyenne of critical race issues in TESOL and Applied Linguistics, voiced her concern with pushing the envelope too much when it comes to LGBTQ+ issues, especially for practitioners in, or students from, national contexts that are typically more socially conservative. During my CCCC's presentation, a similar concern was voiced by one of the audience members (Paiz and Reid 2019).

While I understand where these individuals are coming from, the response bothers me. It bothers me because it suggests that because something is hard to do, we should not do it. Because certain conversations are difficult, sticky, and likely to offend, we should not have them; that we should just accept the silencing of LGBTQ+ voices, the oppression of LGBTQ+ bodies, and the invisibility of LGBTQ+ lives merely because of the current state of ideological affairs and political leanings in a given context. While I firmly acknowledge that such frigid contexts exist, and will give them more space in the Afterword of this book, I still full-throatedly endorsing finding space for LGBTQ+ issues and content in our classes because these issues matter and these students matter. Moreover, even in socially conservative contexts, there are ways to make LGBTQ+ relevant and accessible (see Güney 2019). And, again, in any context, queer inquiry-based pedagogy does not advocate for the rapid evangelizing of

LGBTQ+ inclusivity. It is not a campaign of hearts and minds; it is about awareness raising and moving the needle towards greater access and inclusion (Krause 2017).

Future Directions

This book, the recommendations made within it, and the theories upon which they have been based all come from a growing body of research and scholarship in the subfields of Queer TESOL and Lavender ALx. The past two decades have brought about increased awareness of the role of sexuality in second language learning and acquisition. Despite this fact, there is much that we as a field still do not know. To that end, it is important to outline some of the future directions that may be taken in Queer TESOL/Lavender ALx, as these future directions may inform revisions to your queer inquiry-based pedagogy.

An Increased Understanding of Transgender Issues

Throughout this book, I have attempted to give room to trans voices and issues and their impacts on ELT. One area where we, as a discipline, just do not know enough is in how transgender considerations play out in the classroom or the effects of transgender concerns on second language acquisition processes. I acknowledge that for researchers there are problems gaining access to transgender participants. I am also aware that trans experiences, like lesbian, gay, bisexual, and queer ones, are not universal. There is no single trans experience, nor a single normative trans body. Rather, there are many experiences of and ways of being transgender—some more visible than others. Moreover, transgender populations often represent a marginalized part of an already marginalized population. Taken together, these contribute to a disciplinary blind spot. However, as a discipline, we are also complicit in perpetuating silence around transgender lives and issues and not adequately including them in our theorizing about LGBTQ+ issues and their impacts on ELT.

Therefore, there is a need for the discipline to make a concerted effort to remediate this situation. To not only attempt to better understand transgender concerns and what they mean for our students and our teachers, but also for us to acknowledge a rampant cisgender bias in the field. In

1992, Cynthia Nelson, speaking at a panel at the TESOL annual convention reminded the attendees that we, LGBTQ+-identified individuals, are here. We are part of the field. We are your colleagues, your peers, your friends. And, while our struggles are different from those of our straight peers, we are invested in many of the same goals—even if the field would render us invisible by assuming that we are all straight. It is time for TESOL and Applied Linguistics to acknowledge transgender lives. To makes space for them in our disciplinary meetings. To acknowledge their voices in our literature. And, it is time for these fields to account for them in our understanding of language learning, teaching, acquisition, and use. For too long, we have ignored transgender issues and the challenges that our transgender colleagues face. In rendering them invisible, we have contributed to their silencing and the linguistic violence that they can face in our assemblies, our institutions, and our classrooms. We must acknowledge that our transgender peers are with us, and they are our colleagues and our students. And, we must work together to advocate for the unique needs of transgender practitioners and students—needs to which our cis-privilege may blind us.

Developing Classroom Resources

Throughout this book, I have sought to equip you with the tools and habits-of-mind that you would need to queer your classroom practice. However, as chapter four so clearly showed, curricular materials like texts and textbooks play essential roles in our classroom practice. They are scaffolds for our students as they come to understand the target culture. They are inputs for them as they come to make sense of the target language. And, for new and experienced practitioners alike, they serve as vital supports for classroom planning and teaching. What is currently lacking, however, are dedicated classroom resources that address the intersection of sexuality and ELT. There are few LGBTQ+ lessons or supplemental materials available that are designed for language learners, and next to none that I am aware of that are accessible to different proficiency levels of students.

Therefore, we need to support the development of LGBTQ+-inclusive educational resources—texts, textbooks, supplemental materials, videos, lesson plans, etc.—that can be used by teachers and students across the globe. These resources must be accessible to students of a range of proficiency levels and cover a range of topics (e.g. relationships, family, health, safety, etc.). Additionally, these resources must acknowledge the variance that exists in global queer experiences. That is, instead of presenting LGBTQ+ issues as monolithic and Western, they must acknowledge and celebrate the variegated and global nature of queer experiences. Finally, the development of these materials must be supported from the bottom-up and the top-down. That is, we need space for educators across the globe to develop and share these resources in readily accessible formats, ideally as OERs (bottom-up). However, we also need these resources and their development to be supported by our professional organizations and presses, either through commissioning published works that have resources that teachers can use in their classroom or by the furnishing of grants for practitioners to develop and share these resources (top-down).

Capturing and Analysing Student Experiences

We know a decent bit about our LGBTQ+-identified students and their motivations for acquiring English and Englishes' roles in performing their queer identities. However, we know far less about how our students, both LGBTQ+ and straight, experience and navigate queer educational spaces. Additional research is desperately needed in this area so that we can better inform the ethical queering of our classroom spaces. To date, only a short classroom experiences article in *TESOL Journal* has sought to address this issue directly (Paiz and Zhu 2018). However, this one article is based on only one student's experiences in one queered classroom during one semester of study. We need more systematic interrogations of this phenomenon to inform our theorizing and practice. This research must make space for a range of student experiences and reactions, from those that embrace queer inclusive spaces to those that reject them. Only by accounting for diverse experiences can we have a fuller understanding of the effects, both positive and negative, of a queered classroom practice. Additionally, I would encourage us to find research and publication avenues that make space available for students' voices of their experiences in queered classroom spaces. Once we have made space for and come to understand these experiences, we will be better situated to make recommendations for practice that go beyond those discussed in this book.

Incorporating Queer TESOL/ALx into Teacher Education

Teachers across the globe feel under-prepared to address LGBTQ+ issues in their classrooms (MacDonald 2015; Merse 2017). Additionally, teachers report feeling nervous about incorporating queer themes and content out of worries about how others will respond to their efforts (Saunston 2018). Therefore, teacher education programmes need to more directly engage with the research and scholarship coming out of the subfields of Queer TESOL and Lavender ALx. Only by including queer scholarship from the field in our teacher education courses can we begin to redress the feelings of discomfort and unreadiness that our teachers feel (Paiz 2018, 2019). While the body of literature is small, it is growing; and, it addresses experiences from across the globe. By engaging with this body of work, teacher educators can begin to make the importance of LGBTQ+ lives and issues more salient to novice teachers. By demystifying LGBTQ+ issues and their impacts on language teaching and learning, teacher educators can help to train a new generation of teachers that are better situated to address broader issues of social justice, equity, and inclusion.

A Word of Encouragement and Hope

Often, critical approaches to ELT are maligned as being devoid of hope because they always problematize the world in which they operate (see Pennycook 2001). And, when we engage in a restive problematizing, we find problems. We find inequality. It can create the impression of a bleak picture. This is often because what is missing from that picture is hope. By working to make your classroom more LGBTQ+-inclusive, by engaging with this text and developing your own queer inquiry-based pedagogy, I believe that you are showing the positive sides of critical approaches. For once we find ways to apply them in our practice, we can advocate for our students; we can help them to find a voice; and, we can help them to know that they have a place in our classes. Simply put, once we start to apply what we have gained from critical approaches to ELT, we can find ways to bring hope into our classrooms. And, bringing hope to our students who have felt silenced, marginalized, and ignored is fantastic, uplifting, and transformative for us all.

Afterword: A Special Note on Frigid Contexts

In the inaugural issue of the *Journal of Gender and Power*, Joanna Pawelczyk, Łukasz Pakuła, and Jane Sunderland (2014) addressed issues of power and access in English language classrooms in the traditionally defined foreign language context. Their focus was on how power is felt in relation to issues of gender and sexuality. In this piece, they acknowledge the challenges of making classrooms more LGBTQ+ and gender inclusive and how these challenges are compounded in what has come to be termed *frigid contexts.* Frigid contexts are those spaces were citizens and foreign nationals may face sanctions ranging from expulsion from the community, a lowered social credit score, arrest, or even execution for non-normative gender or sexual identities. In such contexts, often labelled somewhat benignly as 'socially conservative', sexuality is heavily policed in the name of social stability or religious piety. These contexts may include places like Russia, Nigeria, Cameroon, Saudi Arabia, Iraq, Malaysia, and so on; and, are often governed by a set of laws or customs that criminalize same-sex and gender non-conforming lives and bodies.

In such contexts, queering the classroom can be difficult, if not impossible, to do. I acknowledge, with a heavy heart, that such places exist—places where gay, lesbian, and transgender bodies are broken down in the name of remediation; where gay, lesbian, and transgender lives are destroyed in the name of social order. As strongly as I believe in what I have written in this book, as firmly as I trust in its transformative potential, the pedagogical approaches advocated for in this book are not appropriate for all contexts. If including LGBTQ+ readings would lead to termination, harassment, arrest, or loss of life, I would advise against using them.

That being said, we do not live in a world of absolutes. And, even in frigid contexts, there are spots where the social ice of so-called 'conservativism' is thawing. In these places where a thaw is setting in, there is room to queer the classroom in less explicit ways. And, while in frigid contexts we may not be able to directly tell our LGBTQ+ students that they are safe with us, that they have a voice with us, that they can be themselves with us—because we must acknowledge that our classrooms are not cut off from the outside world—we can find ways to challenge students thinking about other aspects of social life. For example, as gender equality becomes a topic of national debate in many contexts where inequality was previously a given, the door is open for us to begin queering our classroom by critically engaging with that moment alongside our students. What is important to remember about queer inquiry-based pedagogies is that while their primary goal is to make the classroom more LGBTQ+ inclusive, these pedagogies are founded on a restive problematizing of *all normative identities*. In frigid contexts, it may be more about planting the seed by troubling students' normative views of less policed identities—perhaps even about the social role of the teacher and of education.

Even with this proviso about frigid contexts, I still believe in the potential of critical and queer pedagogical approaches to transform our students' lives, to make them feel heard, to empower them to advocate for themselves and others. For me, frigid contexts do not represent a veritable 'no-fly zone'. Rather, they require a deft hand in finding those spaces that can be troubled, that can be queered, if even indirectly. Moreover, I believe Paulo Freire (1972) is correct in pointing to education as an agent of change. And, I would echo him in saying that change does happen—even in conservative and frigid national contexts.

Here, I turn to my experiences living and working in the People's Republic of China. In my three years there, I came to experience two queer Chinas: The queer China of the Party and the queer China of the People. Often, these two queer Chinas were divergent in their desires and goals. However, they often influenced each other in profound ways that hold the promise for long term change for the better. For example, in 2016 Beijing released a mandate that there could be no more openly LGBTQ+ characters in web dramas or TV shows. Organizations found in violation would face sanction and potentially have their broadcast licenses pulled (Ellis-Petersen 2016). However, that same year saw the release of a sexual health and education textbook that included a science-based discussion of LGBTQ+ lives in a positive light (Ng 2017). And, during the 2017 China Thinks Big competition, hosted by Harvard University at New York University – Shanghai, I judged 25 student projects, 10 of which sought to address LGBTQ+ inclusion and understanding at the city or provincial levels. While Westerners tend to view China as a country of absolutes, when the people raise their voices the government sometimes has no choice but to listen and change is possible, even if the degree of success is not as far as an observer from a more 'progressive' context might like. But, change in more 'conservative' contexts takes time—a fact we must respect.

However, that does not mean that we stop advocating for change. It does not mean that we do not equip our students for the day when they need to advocate for themselves and others. It does not mean that we do not provide them with the tools to be critical in and across multiple languages. It does not mean that we do not honour and respect the good parts of tradition and heritage while calling into question those that oppress, silence, or render invisible. We must push back. We must equip our students to advocate for themselves and others. We must show them that change is possible—if not in the near term than in the long term.

And, yes, some of our students may choose to leave for more socially progressive settings where they can live their lives unharassed and for them being able to perform a queer self in a second language will be essential for interpersonal connections and acculturations. But, even for our students who will never leave their home contexts, coming face to face with normativity and being equipped with the linguistic and rhetorical skills and the habits-of-mind needed to challenge normativity in all its forms is a vital skill that can carve out space for traditionally marginalized groups—and not just sexual minorities.

At the end of the day, the choice is yours. I would never presume to know all the challenges that you will face. And, if making your classroom more LGBTQ+ inclusive will land you in prison for countless years, I would advise against it because I do not believe in martyrs for a cause. However, I would encourage you to consider what you can use here, to reflect on the pedagogical approach advocated for throughout this book and how parts of it may be used to help drive incremental change. Because, even if our LGBTQ+ students only feel safe when they are with us, if they only feel respected in our classroom and nowhere else—even if they cannot loudly profess their LGBTQ+ identity—at least we have given them temporary respite from the hatred and uncertainty that they may face when they are not with us. Do not underestimate the importance of that momentary peace of mind. It is powerful for our students. It facilitates learning; and, it can be a catalyst for incremental change in individual lives or communities.

Notes

Chapter 2

1 For an overview, see Rowlett and King (2018); or for a state of the art view, see Saunston (2017).

2 For the application of the *comfort zone* metaphor to learning more broadly, see Aldrich (2004), Anderson and Gold (2009), Brown (2008), and Gibson, Hauf, Long, & Simpson (2011).

3 Here, * is being used as a wildcard slot, in which you can place things like 'views towards the family', 'ways of using language to tease/bully', etc.

4 Krause (2017) provides a cogent, yet brief, discussion of some of the issues that can arise when we try to untangle 'queer' for our students when we are in the process of queering our classroom.

Chapter 3

1 Please see the Afterword for an important note on hostile environments and queering the English language classroom.

2 Bangert (2018) discusses how a US national news outlet (Fox News) went into meltdown mode over changes to the Purdue Online Writing Lab (owl.purdue.edu) that included guidelines on using inclusive language in professional and technical communication.

3 Per a *Google Trends* analysis conducted on 30 January 2019 (see https://trends.google.com/trends/explore?date=all_2008&gprop=news&q=%2Fm%2F0hn10).

4 This number is based on a quick and dirty analysis of publicly available enrollment information from North American, and Sino-American joint venture universities. I acknowledge in many EFL contexts, these numbers are much higher.

5 LGBT History Month offers a wealth of resources that can be deployed in the classroom: https://lgbthistorymonth.com/resources

6 Pronoun stickers can easily be made at home using Avery 8167 or 5260 labels. Alternatively, they can be purchased online through various shops like Etsy (www.etsy.com/market/pronoun_stickers).

Chapter 4

1 For one example, see the relationship abuse infographic used by Harry S. Truman High School (2016) in New York City, USA.

References

Adler-Kassner, Linda. 2008. *Activist WPA: The Changing Stories About Writing and Writers.* Logan, UT: Utah State University Press.

Alber, Rebecca. 2013. 5 Powerful Questions Teachers Can Ask Students. Edutopia. Accessed 5 March 2019. www.edutopia.org/blog/five-powerful-questions-teachers-ask-students-rebecca-alber

Aldrich, Clark. 2004. *Simulations and the Future of Learning: An Innovative (and Perhaps Revolutionary) Approach to e-Learning.* San Francisco, CA: Pfeiffer.

Alexander, Jonathan. 2008. *Literacy, Sexuality, Pedagogy: Theory and Practice for Composition Studies.* Logan, UT: Utah State University Press.

Allen, Samantha. 2017. How Trump Made 2017 a Horrific Year for LGBT Rights—And Worse is Yet to Come. *The Daily Beast.* Accessed on 29 January 2018. www.thedailybeast.com/how-trump-made-2017-a-horrific-year-for-lgbt-rightsand-worse-is-to-come.

Anderson, Jason. 2018. Reimagining English Language Learners from a Translingual Perspective. *ELT Journal* 72, no. 1: 26–37. https://doi.org/10.1093/elt/ccx029

Anderson, Lisa and Jeff Gold. 2009. Conversations Outside the Comfort Zone: Identity Formation in SME Manager Action Learning. *Action Learning: Research and Practice* 6, no. 3: 229–242. https://doi.org/10.1080/14767330903299449

Appiah, Kwame Anthony. 2007. Global Citizenship. *Fordham Law Review* 75, no. 5: 2375–2391.

Apple, Michael and Linda Christian-Smith. 1991. *The Politics of the Textbook.* New York: Routledge.

Aspinwall, Nick. 2019. Taiwan Inches Closer to Marriage Equality with New Draft Bill. *The Diplomat.* Last modified 28 February 2019. https://thediplomat.com/2019/03/taiwan-inches-closer-to-marriage-equality-with-new-draft-bill.

Assemblies of God. 2019. Homosexuality, Marriage, and Sexual Identity. https://ag.org/Beliefs/Position-Papers/Homosexuality-Marriage-and-Sexual-Identity.

Atkinson, Dwight. 1997. A Critical Approach to Critical Thinking in TESOL. *TESOL Quarterly* 31, no. 1: 71–94.

Atkinson, Dwight. 2002. Towards a Sociocognitive Approach to Second Language Acquisition. *Modern Language Journal* 86, no. 4: 535–545. https://doi.org/10.1111/1540-4781.00159

Atkinson, Dwight. 2011. *Alternative Approaches to Second Language Acquisition*. New York: Routledge.

Atkinson, Dwight. 2016. Second Language Writing and Culture. In *Handbook of Second and Foreign Language Writing*, edited by Rosa M. Manchon and Paul Kei Matsuda, 544–564. Berlin: De Gruyter.

Atkinson, Dwight and Jija Sohn. 2013. Culture from the Bottom Up. *TESOL Quarterly* 47, no. 4: 669–693. https://doi.org/10.1002/tesq.104

Atkinson, Dwight, Eton Churchill, Takako Nishino, and Hanako Okada. 2007. Alignment and Interaction in a Sociocognitive Approach to Second Language Acquisition. *Modern Language Journal* 91, no. 2: 169–188. https://doi.org/10.1111/1540-4781.2007.00539.x

Ball, D. L. and S. Feiman-Nemser. 1988. Using Textbooks and Teacher's Guides: A Dilemma for Beginning Teachers and Teacher Educators. *Curriculum Inquiry* 18, no. 4: 401–423.

Bangert, Dave. 2018. Ban on 'Man'? Purdue Silent as Conservative Media Rips on Writing Guidelines. *Journal & Courier.* Last modified 2 March 2018. www.jconline.com/story/opinion/columnists/dave-bangert/2018/02/26/bangert-ban-man-purdue-silent-conservative-media-rips-writing-guidelines/375820002.

Banville, Sean. 2017. English Discussion on Gay Rights. Last modified 2017. https://breakingnewsenglish.com/help.html.

Barnard, Ian. 1994. Anti-Homophobic Pedagogy: Some Suggestions for Teachers. *Radical Teacher* 45: 26–28.

Barrett, Peter, Yufan Zhang, Joanne Moffat, and Khairy Kobbacy. 2013. A Holistic, Multi-level Analysis Identifying the Impact of Classroom Design on Pupils' Learning. *Building and Environment* 59: 678–689. https://doi.org/10.1016/buildenv.2012.09.016

Barrett, Peter, Fay Davies, Yufan Zhang, and Lucinda Barrett. 2015. The Impact of Classroom Design on Pupils' Learning: Final Results of a Holistic, Multi-level Analysis. *Building and Environment* 89: 118–133. https://doi.org/10.1016/buildenv.2015.02.013

Bator, Paul. 1980. Aristotelian and Rogerian Rhetoric. *College Composition and Communication* 31, no. 4: 427–432. https://doi.org/10.2307/356593

Bearak, Max. 2019. Kenya is Closer to Legalizing Homosexuality. What About the Rest of Africa? *The Washington Post.* Last modified 22 February 2019. www.washingtonpost.com/world/2019/02/21/kenya-is-close-legalizing-homosexuality-what-about-rest-africa/?utm_term=.33ac962d792f.

Beatty, Ken. 2013. *LEAP Advanced*. New York: Pearson.

Bennett, M. 2013. *Basic Concepts of Intercultural Communication: Paradigms, Principles, and Practices*. Boston, MA: Intercultural Press.

Blewett, Kelly, Janine Morris, and Hannah J. Rule. 2013. Composing Environments: The Materiality of Reading and Writing. *CEA Critic* 78, no. 1: 24–44. https://doi.org/10.1353/cea.2016.0007

Block, David. 2003. *The Social Turn in Second Language Acquisition*. Edinburgh: Edinburgh University Press.

Block, David. 2007. *Second Language Identities*. London: Continuum.

Blythe, Stuart. 2001. Designing Online Courses: User-Centered Principles. *Computers and Composition* 18, no. 4: 329–346.

Board of Trustees. 2014. Mission Statement. www.liberty.edu/index.cfm?PID=6899.

Boroff, David. 2018, March 28. Elementary School Teacher in Texas Suspended After Parent Complains of Her 'Homosexual Agenda': Lawyer. *Daily News*. Accessed on 7 March 2019. www.nydailynews.com/news/national/teacher-suspended-homosexual-agenda-lawyer-claims-article-1.3901664

Brenner, Gail, Marsha Ford, and Patricia Sullivan, eds. 2007. *Celebrate! Holidays in the USA*. 2nd ed. Washington, DC: United States Department of State.

Bristow, Joseph. 2011. *Sexuality: The New Critical Idiom*. 2nd ed. New York: Routledge.

Britzman, Deborah P. 1995. Is There a Queer Pedagogy? Or, Stop Reading Straight. *Educational Theory* 45, no. 2: 151–165.

Brooke, Robert. 1987. Underlife and writing instruction. *College Composition and Communication* 38, no. 2: 141–153.

Brown, Mike. 2008. Comfort Zone: Model or Metaphor? *Australian Journal of Outdoor Education* 12, no. 1: 3–12.

Butler, Judith. 1990. *Gender Trouble: Feminism and the Subversion of Identity*. New York: Routledge.

Cahnmann-Taylor, Melisa and James Coda. 2018. Troubling Normal in World Language Education. *Critical Inquiry in Language Studies* 16, no. 2: 1–23. https://doi.org/10.1080/15427587.2018.1450632

Cameron, Deborah. 2005. Language, Gender and Sexuality: Current Issues and New Directions. *Applied Linguistics* 26, no. 4: 482–502. https://doi.org/10.1093/applin/ami027

Canagarajah, Suresh. 2013. *Translingual Practice: Global Englishes and Cosmopolitan Relations*. London: Routledge.

Carlson, Jennifer. 2018. *Wide Angle: Level 1*. Oxford, UK: Oxford University Press.

Carr, Jo and Anne Pauwels. 2006. *Boys and Foreign Language Learning: Real Boys Don't Do Languages*. New York: Palgrave Macmillan.

Carscadden, Lisa, Jim Ward, and Cynthia D. Nelson. 1992. We Are Your Colleagues: Lesbians and Gays in ESL. Colloquium presentation, 26th Annual TESOL Convention, Vancouver, CA.

Casanave, Christine Pearson and Xiaoming Li, eds. 2008. *Learning the Literacy Practices of Graduate School: Insiders' Reflections on Academic Enculturation.* Ann Arbor, MI: University of Michigan Press.

Centers for Disease Control and Prevention. 2017. LGBT Youth. Last modified June 2017. www.cdc.gov/lgbthealth/youth.htm.

Chack, Erin. 2014. 21 Pointlessly Gendered Products. Last modified on 24 January 2014. www.buzzfeed.com/erinchack/pointlessly-gendered-products.

Cheryan, Sapna, Victoria C. Plaut, Caitlin Handron, and Lauren Hudson. 2012. The Stereotypical Computer Scientist: Gendered Media Representations as a Barrier to Inclusion for Women. *Sex Roles* 69, no. 1–2: 58–71. https://doi.org/10.1007/s11199-013-0296-x

Cho, Seonhee. 2013. Disciplinary Enculturation Experiences of Three Korean Students in US-based MATESOL Programs. *Journal of Language, Identity, and Education* 12, no. 2: 135–151. https://doi.org/10.1080/15348458.2013.775881

Chory, Rebecca M. and Evan H. Offstein. 2016. 'Your Professor Will Know You as a Person': Evaluating and Rethinking the Boundaries between Faculty and Students. *Journal of Management Education* 41, no. 1: 9–38. https://doi.org/10.1177/1052562916647986

Christison, Maryann and Denise E. Murray. 2009. *Leadership in English Language Education: Theoretical Foundations and Practical Skills for Changing Times.* New York: Routledge.

Churchill, Eton. 2007. A Dynamic Systems Account of Learning a Word: From Ecology to Form Relations. *Applied Linguistics* 29, no. 3: 339–358. https://doi.org/10.1093/applin/amm019

Coda, James. 2018a. Disrupting Standard Practice: Queering the World Language Classroom. *Dimension* 2018: 74–89.

Coda, James. 2018b. Queering TESOL and World Language Pedagogy: Troubling Norms and Finding Trouble. Colloquium presentation, Meeting of the American Association for Applied Linguistics, Chicago, IL.

Coleman, Douglas W. and Joshua M. Paiz. 2010 'Let's Stop Teaching Our Students to Sound Foreign. Paper presented at the Ohio TESOL Convention, Columbus, OH.

Coleman, Douglas W. and Kasumi Yamazaki. 2018. Simulation. In *The TESOL Encyclopedia of English Language Teaching*, edited by John I. Liontas and Margo DelliCarpini. Hoboken, NJ: Wiley Blackwell.

Collopy, Rachel. 2003. Curriculum Materials as a Professional Development Tool: How a Mathematics Textbook Affected Two Teacher's Experiences. *The Elementary School Journal* 10, no. 3: 287–311. https://doi.org/10.1086/499727

Craig, Shelley L., Lauren McInroy, Lance T. McCready, and Ramona Alaggia. 2015. Media: A Catalyst for Resilience in Lesbian, Gay, Bisexual, Transgender, and Queer Youth. *Journal of LGBT Youth* 12, no. 3: 254–275. https://doi.org/10.1080/19361653.2015.1040193

Curran, Greg. 2002. Young Queers Getting Together: Moving Beyond Isolation and Loneliness. Unpublished doctoral dissertation, University of Melbourne, Melbourne.

Curran, Greg. 2006. Responding to Students' Normative Questions about Gays: Putting Queer Theory into Practice in an Australian ESL Classroom [The Forum]. *Journal of Language, Identity, & Education* 5, no. 1: 85–96. https://doi.org/10.1207/s15327701jlie0501_6

Davies, Ian and Graham Pike. 2009. Global Citizenship Education: Challenges and Possibilities. In *The Handbook of Practice and Research in Study Abroad*, edited by Ross Lewin, 61–78. New York: Routledge.

Deters, Ping. 2011. *Identity, Agency, and the Acquisition of Professional Language and Culture*. London: Continuum.

De Vincenti, Gloria, Angela Giovanangeli, and Rowena Ward. 2007. The Queer Stopover: How Queer Travels in the Language Classroom. *Electronic Journal of Foreign Language Teaching* 4, no. 1: 58–72.

Dick, Jeffery. 1997. The Learner-Centered Environment: Using the 'Fat L' Shaped Classroom. Paper presented at the Environmental Design Research Association Conference, Montreal, Canada.

Dörnyei, Zoltán and Ema Uchida, eds. 2009. *Motivation, Language, Identity, and L2 Self*. Bristol: Multilingual Matters.

Duggan, Lisa. 2002. The New Homonormativity: The Sexual Politics of Neoliberalism. In *Materializing Democracy: Toward a Revitalized Cultural Politics*, edited by Russ Castronovo and Dana Nelson, 175–194. Durham, NC: Duke University Press. https://doi.org/10.1215/978008223901

Durso, Laura E. and Gary J. Gates. 2012. *Serving our Youth: Findings from a National Survey of Service Providers Working with Lesbian, Gay, Bisexual, and Transgender Youth Who are Homeless or at Risk of Becoming Homeless*. Los Angeles, CA: The Williams Institute with True Colors Fund and The Palette Fund.

Edge, Julian. 2011. *The Reflexive Teacher Educator in TESOL: Roots and Wings*. New York: Routledge.

Ellis-Petersen, Hannah. 2016. China Bans Depictions of Gay People on TV. *The Guardian*, 4 March. Accessed on 18 March 2019. www.theguardian.com/tv-and-radio/2016/mar/04/china-bans-gay-people-television-clampdown-xi-jinping-censorship

Equality Challenge Unit. 2015. Academic Flight: How to Encourage Black and Minority Ethnic Academics to Stay in UK Higher Education. White paper, Equality Challenge Unit, Liverpool.

Erlman, Lisa. 2015. Heteronormativity in EFL Textbooks: A Review of the Current State of Research on Gender-Bias and Heterosexism in ELT Reading Material. Unpublished C-thesis, Göteborg Universitet, Gothenburg.

Eschelbach Hansen, Mary. 2006. *The Value of Adoption.* American University Department of Economics Working Papers Series, American University, Washington, DC. Accessed on 12 March 2019. http://citeseerx.ist.psu.edu/viewdoc/download?doi=10.1.1.686.764&rep=rep1&type=pdf

Esseks, James D. 2017. Anti-Trans Bathroom Bills Have Nothing to do with Privacy and Everything to do with Fear and Hatred. *Huffpost Blog.* Last modified on 16 April 2017. www.huffingtonpost.com/james-d-esseks/anti-trans-bathroom-bills_b_9703224.html?utm_hp_ref=queer-voices.

Eyewitness News. 2018. Gay Teacher Fired after Posting Her Wedding Photos Online. *ABC 13 Eyewitness News*, 10 February. Accessed on 7 March 2019. https://abc13.com/society/gay-teacher-fired-after-posting-her-wedding-photos-online/3064413

Fraiberg, Steven, Xiqiao Wang, and Xiaoye You. 2017. *Inventing the World Grant University: Chinese Students' Mobilities, Literacies, and Identities.* Logan, UT: Utah State University Press.

Francis, Simone., I-Yi Hsieh, and Joshua M. Paiz. 2017. Creating welcoming Classrooms: Diversity and Inclusion in Teaching. NYU Shanghai Teaching and Lunching Panel Discussions, NYU Shanghai Office of Faculty Affairs, Shanghai, China.

Freire, Paulo. 1972. *Pedagogy of the Oppressed.* London: Penguin.

Gaines, Kristi S. and Zane D. Curry. 2011. The Inclusive Classroom: The Effects of Color on Learning and Behavior. *Journal of Family & Consumer Sciences Education* 29, no. 1: 46–57.

Gherwash, Ghada and Joshua M. Paiz. n.d. Building Online Writing Labs: Developing Effective Online L2 Writing Instructional Support. Unpublished research manuscript, Belgrade, ME.

Gibson, Murray, Petra Hauf, Brad S. Long, and Gina Sampson. 2011. Reflective Practices in Service Learning: Possibilities and Limitations. *Education + Training* 53, no. 4: 284–296. https://doi.org/10.1108/00400911111138451

GLAAD. n.d. Transgender FAQ. Retrieved from www.glaad.org/transgender/transfaq.

GLSEN. 2011. *The 2011 National School Climate Survey: The Experiences of Lesbian, Gay, Bisexual, and Transgender Youth in our Nation's Schools.* New York: GLSEN.

GLSEN. 2017. *The 2017 National School Climate Survey: The Experiences of Lesbian, Gay, Bisexual, and Transgender Youth in our Nation's Schools.* New York: GLSEN.

GLSEN. n.d. That's a (Gender) Stereotype. Retrieved from www.glsen.org/article/thats-gender-stereotype.

Grant, Rachel, Ryuko Kubota, Angel Lin, Suhanthie Motha, Gertrude Tinker Sachs, and Stephanie Vandrick. 2019. Collaboration, Polyvocality, and Social Justice: Women of Color in Academia. Panel presented at the 2019 TESOL International Association Conference, Atlanta, GA, March.

Gray, John. 2013. LGBT Invisibility and Heteronormativity in ELT Materials. In *Critical Perspectives on Language Teaching Materials*, edited by John Gray, 40–63. New York: Palgrave Macmillan.

Green, Warren and Barbara Levy Simon, eds. 2012. *The Columbia Guide to Social Work Writing*. New York: Columbia University Press.

Grossman, Arnold H. and Anthony R. D'Augelli. 2006. Transgender Youth: Invisible and Vulnerable. *Journal of Homosexuality* 51, no. 5: 111–128.

Grossman, Pam and Clarissa Thompson. 2008. Learning from Curricular Materials: Scaffolds for New Teachers? *Teaching and Teacher Education* 24: 2014–2026. https://doi.org/10.1016/j.tate.2008.05.002

Güney, Ozge. 2019. Queering Teacher Education Programs: Perceptions of Pre-service EFL Teachers towards Queer Issues. Paper presented at the 2019 Conference of the American Association for Applied Linguistics, Atlanta, GA, March.

Halpern, Diane F. 2013. *Thought and Knowledge: An Introduction to Critical Thinking*. 5th ed. New York: New York University Press.

Hancock, Penny. 2008. *Love in the Lakes*. Cambridge: Cambridge University Press.

Harry S. Truman High School. 2016. Dating Abuse. Retrieved from www.bxtrumanhighschool.com/2016/10/20/october-is-domestic-violence-awareness-month/788b719264d349b53494e368d0e906b9/

Hartmann, Pamela and Laurie Blass. 2007. *Quest Intro: Reading and Writing*. 2nd ed. New York: McGraw Hill.

Hassett, Dawnene D. and Melissa B. Schieble. 2010. Finding Time For the Visual in K-12 Literacy Instruction. In *Contemporary Readings in Literacy Education*, edited by Marva Cappello and Barbara Moss, 325–332. Thousand Oaks, CA: SAGE Publications.

Hawkins, Margaret and Bonny Norton. 2009. Critical Language Teacher Education. In *Cambridge Guide to Second Language Teacher Education*, edited by Anne Burns and Jack C. Richards, 30–39. New York: Cambridge University Press.

Healy, Karen and Joan Mulholland. 2012. *Writing Skills for Social Workers*. 2nd ed. Thousand Oaks, CA: Sage Publishing.

Herthel, Jessica and Jazz Jennings. 2014. *I Am Jazz*. New York: Dial Books.

Hogan, John. 2018. Michigan Lawmakers Want to End Gender Classification of Fast-Food Toys. *Detroit Free Press*. Last modified on 28 November 2018. www.freep.com/story/news/politics/2018/11/28/fast-food-toys-gender-classification/2140125002/.

Housego, Elizabeth and Christine Burns. 1994. Are You Sitting Comfortably? A Critical Look at 'Circle Time' in the Primary Classroom. *English in Education* 28, no. 2: 23–30. https://doi.org/10.1111/j.1754-8845.1994.tb01117.x

Human Rights Campaign. 2017. Violence Against the Transgender Community in 2017. Last modified in 2018. www.hrc.org/resources/violence-against-the-transgender-community-in-2017.

Human Rights Watch. 2016. 'Like Walking through a Hailstorm': Discrimination against LGBT Youth in US Schools. Human Rights Watch Online. Accessed 6 March 2019. www.hrw.org/report/2016/12/07/walking-through-hailstorm/discrimination-against-lgbt-youth-us-schools#page

Hyland, Ken. 2004. *Disciplinary Discourses: Social Interactions in Academic Writing.* Ann Arbor, MI: University of Michigan Press.

Ibrahim, Awad El Karim M. 1999. Becoming Black: Rap, Hip-Hop, Race, gender, Identity, and the Politics of ESL Learning. *TESOL Quarterly* 33, no. 3: 349–369.

Ibrahim, Tasneem. 2005. Global Citizenship Education: Mainstreaming the Curriculum? Cambridge Journal of Education 35, no. 2: 177–194. https://doi.org/10.1080/03057640500146823

Ignatavicius, Stephanie. 2013. Stress in Female-Identified Transgender Youth: A Review of Literature on Effects and Interventions. *Journal of LGBT Youth* 10, no. 4: 267–286.

Jagose, Annamarie. 1996. *Queer Theory: An Introduction.* New York: New York University Press.

Jin, Ha. 2001. *The Bridegroom.* New York: Vintage Books.

Jin, Ha. 2012. In Defense of Foreignness. In *The Routledge Handbook of World Englishes*, edited by Andy Kirkpatrick, 461–470. New York, Routledge.

Jones, Ken. 1982. *Simulations in Language Teaching.* Cambridge: Cambridge University Press.

Kachru, Braj B. 1990. *The Alchemy of English: The Spread, Functions, and Models of Non-Native Englishes.* Reprint ed. Urbana, IL: University of Illinois Press.

Kachru, Braj B. 2006. Standards, Codification and Sociolinguistic Realism: The English Language in the Outer Circle. In *World Englishes: Critical Concepts in Linguistics*, vol. 3, edited by Kingsley Bolton and Braj B. Kachru, 241–269. New York: Routledge.

Kachru, Yamuna and Cecil L. Nelson. 2006. *World Englishes in Asian Contexts.* Hong Kong: Hong Kong University Press.

Kaiser, Evan. 2017. LGBTQ+ Voices from the Classroom: Insights from ESOL Teachers. *CATESOL Journal* 29, no. 1: 1–21.

Kanno, Yasuko. 2003. Imagined Communities, School Visions, and Education of Bilingual Students in Japan. *Journal of Language, Identity, and Education* 2, no. 4: 285–300. https://doi.org/10.1207/S15327701JLIE0204_4

Kanno, Yasuko and Bonny Norton. 2003. Imagined Communities and Educational Possibilities: Introduction. *Journal of Language, Identity, and Education* 2, no. 4: 241–249. https://doi.org/10.1207/S15327701JLIE0204_1

Khayatt, Didi. 2003. Terms of Desire: Are There Lesbians in Egypt? In *Language Socialization in Bilingual and Multilingual Societies*, edited by Robert Bayley and Sandra R. Schecter, 218–233. Clevedon: Multilingual Matters.

King, Brian W. 2008. 'Being Gay Guy, That is the Advantage': Queer Korean Language Learning and Identity Construction. *Journal of Language Identity, and Education* 7, no. 3/4: 230–252. https://doi.org/10.1080/15348450802237855

Knapper, Christopher K. and Arthur J. Cropley. 2000. *Lifelong Learning in Higher Education*. 3rd ed. London, Routledge.

Kramsch, Claire. 2004. Language, Thought, and Culture. In *The Handbook of Applied Linguistics*, edited by Alan Davies and Catherine Elder, 235–254. Oxford: Blackwell.

Kramsch, Claire. 2013. Culture in Foreign Language Teaching. *Iranian Journal of Foreign Language Teaching* 1, no. 1: 57–78.

Krashen, Stephen D. 1985. *The Input Hypothesis: Issues and Implications*. New York: Longman.

Krause, Timothy. 2018. *Home and School: Ten Easy Picture Stories for Beginning Students of English*. Portland, OR: Portland Community College.

Krause, Timothy. 2017. Queering the ESL Classroom: A Case Study. *TESOLers for Social Justice: The Newsletter of the Social Responsibility Interest Section*. Last modified September 2017. http://newsmanager.commpartners.com/tesolsris/issues/2017-09-21/4.html.

Krug, Steve. 2009. *Rocket Surgery Made Easy: The Do-It-Yourself Guide to Finding and Fixing Usability Problems*. San Francisco, CA: New Riders.

Kubota, Ryuko and Angel Lin. 2006. Race and TESOL: Introduction to Concepts and Theories. *TESOL Quarterly* 40, no. 3: 471–493. https://doi.org/10.2307/40264540

Kubota, Ryuko and Yilin Sun, eds. 2013. *Demystifying Career Paths After Graduate School: A Guide for Second Language Professionals in Higher Education*. Charlotte, NC: Information Age Publishing.

Lacina, Jan G. 2002. Preparing International Students for a Successful Social Experience in Higher Education. *New Directions for Higher Education* 117: 21–28. https://doi.org/10.1002/he.43

Lantolf, James and Ali Alijaafreh. 1995. Second Language Learning in the Zone of Proximal Development: Revolutionary Experience. *International Journal of Educational Research* 23, no. 7: 619–632. https://doi.org/10.1016/0883-0355(96)80441-1

Leap, William L. 2013. Commentary II: Queering Language and Normativity. *Discourse & Society* 5, no. 1: 643–648. https://doi.org/10.1177/0957926513490320

Leap, William L. and Heiko Motschenbacher. 2012. Launching a New Phase in Language and Sexuality Studies. *Journal of Language and Sexuality* 1, no. 1: 1–14. https://doi.org/10.1075/jls.1.1.01lea

Leather, Sue. 2003. *Bad Love*. Cambridge: Cambridge University Press.

Levy, Dana Alison. 2015. *The Misadventures of the Family Fletcher*. New York: Yearling Books.

Leyva, Luis, Jacob Massa, and Dan Battey. 2016. Queering Engineering: A Critical Analysis of the Gendered Technical/Social Dualism in Engineering and Engineering Education Research. *Proceedings of the American Society of Engineering Education's 123rd Annual Conference*, paper ID: 17257. New Orleans, LA: ASEE.

LGBT Network. 2019. #WearTheRibbon. http://weartheribbon.org/about-national-coming-out-day-campaign-lgbt-network

LGBTQ Center at UNC. n.d. How to support LGBT students on campus. UNC Student Affairs. Accessed 6 March 2019. https://lgbtq.unc.edu/programs-services/safe-zone/how-to-support-lgbt-students

Liberty University. 2019. Doctrinal Statement. Last modified February 2019. www.liberty.edu/aboutliberty/index.cfm?PID=6907

Liddicoat, Anthony J. 2009. Sexual Identity as Linguistic Failure: Trajectories of Interaction in the Heteronormative Language Classroom. *Journal of Language, Identity, and Education* 8, no. 2–3: 191–202.

Liddicoat, Anthony J. 2018. Language Teaching and Learning as a Transdisciplinary Endeavour. *AILA Review* 31, no. 1: 14–28. https://doi.org/10.1075/aila.00011

Linguistic Society of America. 2018. New Special Interest Group on LGBTQ+ Issues Established. LSA News. Last modified 2018. www.linguisticsociety.org/news/2018/04/05/new-special-interest-group-lgbtq-issues-established.

Liu, Petrus. 2015. *Queer Marxism in Two China*. Dunham, NC: Duke University Press.

Lunsford, Andrea A. 1979. Aristotelian vs. Rogerian Argument: A Reassessment. *College Composition and Communication* 30, no. 2: 146–151. https://doi.org/10.2307/356318

MacDonald, Sheila. 2015. Exploring LGBT Lives and Issues in Adult ESOL: Part One. *Language Issues* 26, no. 1: 43–49.

MacDonald, Sheila, Laila El-Metoui, Mike Baynham, and John Gray. 2014. *Exploring LGBT Lives and Issues in Adult ESOL*. ESOL Nexus Research Awards Report. London: British Council.

Maritz, Jeanette and Paul Prinsloo. 2015. 'Queering' and Querying Academic Identities in Post Graduate Education. *Higher Education Research and*

Development 34, no. 4: 695–708. https://doi.org/10.1080/07294360.2015.1051007

Merse, Thorsten. 2014. Promoting Sexual Literacy through Queer Pedagogy in EFL and ESOL Classrooms: Materials and Methods. Presented at Queering ESOL: Towards a Cultural Politics of LGBT Issues in the ESOL Classroom, Seminar 3: Voices from the Classroom—LGBT Teachers and Learners, 21 June, King's College, London.

Merse, Thorsten. 2015. Queer-Informed Approaches and Sexual Literacy in ETL: Theoretical Foundations and Teaching Principles. *Language Issues* 26, no. 1: 13–20.

Merse, Thorsten. 2017. Other Others, Different Differences: Queer Perspectives on Teaching English as a Foreign Language. Unpublished doctoral dissertation, Ludwig-Maximillian University, Munich.

Miller, Paul Chamness and Hidehiro Endo. 2018. Troubling the Foreign/Second Language Writing Classroom. Presented at Queering TESOL and World Languages Pedagogy: Troubling Norms and Finding Trouble, colloquium organized by James Coda, conducted at the meeting of the American Association for Applied Linguistics, Chicago, IL.

Minning Heidi. 2004. Qwir-English Code-Mixing in Germany: Constructing a Rainbow of Identities. In *Speaking in Queer Tongues: Globalization and Gay Language*, edited by Tom Boellstorff and William L. Leap. Urbana, IL: University of Illinois Press.

Moita-Lopes, Luiz Paulo. 2006. Queering Literacy Teaching: Analyzing Gay-Themed Discourses in a Fifth Grade Class in Brazil. *Journal od Language, Identity, and Education* 5, no. 1: 31–50. https://doi.org/10.1207/s15327701jlie0501_3

Moore, Ashley R. 2013. The Ideal Sexual Self: The Motivational Investments of Japanese Gay Male Learners of English. In *The Applied Linguistic Individual: Sociocultural Approaches to Identity, Agency, and Autonomy*, edited by Phil Benson and Lucky Cooker, 135–151. Sheffield: Equinox Publishing.

Moore, Ashley R. 2016. Inclusion and Exclusion: A Case Study of an English Class for LGBT Learners. *TESOL Quarterly* 50, no. 1: 86–108. https://doi.org/10.1002/tesq208

Morgan, Brian D. 2002. Critical Practice in Community-based ESL Programs: A Canadian Perspective. *Journal of Language Identity, and Education* 1, no. 2: 141–162. https://doi.org/10.1207/S15327701JLIE0102_03

Motschenbacher, Heiko. 2010. *Language, Gender, and Sexual Identity: Poststructuralist Perspectives.* Amsterdam: John Benjamins.

Motschenbacher, Heiko. 2011a. 'Now Everybody can Wear a Skirt': Linguistic Constructions of Non-heteronormativity at Eurovision Song Contest

Press Conferences. *Discourse & Society* 24, no. 5: 590–614. https://doi.org/10.1177/0957926513486167

Motschenbacher, Heiko. 2011b. Taking Queer Linguistics Further: Sociolinguistics and Critical Heteronormativity Research. *International Journal of the Sociology of Language* 212: 149–179. https://doi.org/10.1515/IJSL.2011.050

Motschenbacher, Heiko and Martin Stegu. 2013. Queer Linguistic Approaches to Discourse. *Discourse & Society* 24, no. 5: 519–535. https://doi.org/10.1177/095792651386069

Muckler, Virginia C., Rachel Leonard, and Ethan C. Cicero. 2019. Transgender Simulation Scenario Pilot Project. *Clinical Simulation in Nursing* 26: 44–48. https://doi.org/10.1016/j.ecns.2018.10.007

Mustapha, Abolaji S. 2013. Gender and Language Education Research: A Review. *Journal of Language Teaching and Research* 4, no. 3: 454–463. https://doi.org/10.4304/jltr.4.3.454-463

NCTE. 2016. Understanding Transgender People: The Basics. National Center for Transgender Equality. Accessed 6 March 2019. https://transequality.org/issues/resources/understanding-transgender-people-the-basics

Nelson, Cynthia D. 1993. Heterosexism in ESL: Examining our Attitudes [The Forum]. *TESOL Quarterly* 27, no. 1: 143–150. https://doi.org/10.2307/2586966

Nelson, Cynthia D. 1999. Sexual Identities in ESL: Queer Theory and Classroom Inquiry. *TESOL Quarterly* 33, no. 3: 371–391. https://doi.org/10.2307/3587670

Nelson, Cynthia D. 2002. Why Queer Theory is Useful in Teaching: A Perspective from English as a Second Language. In *From Here to Diversity: Globalization and Intercultural Dialogues*, edited by Clara Sarmento, 43–53. Cambridge: Cambridge University Scholars. https://doi.org/10.1300/j04v14n02_04

Nelson, Cynthia D. 2006. Queer Inquiry in Language Education. *Journal of Language, Identity, and Education* 5, no. 1: 1–9. https://doi.org/10.1207/s15327701jlie0501_1

Nelson, Cynthia D. 2007. Queer Thinking about Language Teaching: An Overview of Published Work. In *Gender Studies and Foreign Language Teaching*, edited by H. Decke-Cornill and L. Volkmann, 63–76. Tubingen: Guten Narr.

Nelson, Cynthia D. 2009. *Sexual Identities in English Language Education: Classroom Conversations.* New York: Routledge.

New Oriental. n.d. What We Do—Language Training. *New Oriental Education & Technology Group.* Accessed 14 March 2019. www.neworiental.org/english/what/language.html

Ng, Yi Shu. 2017. Elementary Sex Education Textbook Marks Leap Forward for Conservative China. *Mashable*, 6 March. Accessed on 18 March 2019. https://mashable.com/2017/03/06/sex-education-textbook-china/#QxMYgfKr.iqB

Nguyen, Hanhthi and Lajlim Yang. 2015. A Queer Learner's Identity Positioning in Second Language Classroom Discourse. *Classroom Discourse* 6, no. 3: 221–241. https://doi.org/10.1080/19463014.2015.1093952

Nicol, Cynthia. 2006. Designing a Pedagogy of Inquiry in Teacher Education: Moving from Resistance to Learning. *Studying Teacher Education* 2, no. 1: 25–41. https://doi.org/10.1080/17425960600557454

Nicol, Cynthia C. and Sandra M. Crespo. 2006. Learning to Teach with Mathematics Textbooks: How Preservice Teachers Interpret and Use Curriculum Materials. *Educational Studies in Mathematics* 62, no. 3: 331–355: https://doi.org/10.1007/s10649-006-5423-y

Norton, Bonny and Anita Pavlenko, eds. 2004. *Gender and English Language Learners.* Alexandria, VA: TESOL Press.

Ó'Móchain, Robert. 2006. Discussing Gender and Sexuality in a Context-appropriate Way: Queer Narratives in an EFL College Classroom in Japan. *Journal of Language, Identity, and Education* 5, no. 1: 51–66. https://doi.org/10.1207/s15327701jlie0501_4

Ortmeier-Hooper, Christina. 2008. 'English May Be My Second Language, but I'm Not "ESL"'. *College Composition and Communication* 59, no. 3: 389–419. https://doi.org/10.1007/springerreference_69911

Paiz, Joshua. M. 2015a. Over the Monochrome Rainbow: Heteronormativity in ESL Reading Texts and Textbooks. *Journal of Language and Sexuality* 4, no. 1: 77–101. https://doi.org/10.1075/jls.4.1.03pai

Paiz, Joshua. M. 2015b. Toward a Sociocognitive Approach to Professional Identity and Professionalization in Applied Linguistics. Unpublished doctoral dissertation, West Lafayette, IN: Purdue University. ProQuest Document ID: 3734499.

Paiz, Joshua. M. 2018. Queering ESL Teaching: Issues of Teacher Training and Materials Creation. *TESOL Journal* 9, no. 2: 348–367. https://doi.org/10.1002/tesj.329

Paiz, Joshua. M. 2019. Queering Practice: LGBTQ+ Diversity and Inclusion in English Language Teaching [The Forum]. *Journal of Language, Identity, and Education* 18 no. 4: 266–275.

Paiz, Joshua. M. 2020a. Introducing LGBTQ+ Issues: Dynamic Classroom Negotiations for ELT Practitioners. In *Linguistic Perspectives on Sexuality in Education: Representations, Constructions, and Negotiations*, edited by Łukasz Pakuła. Basingstoke: Palgrave Macmillan.

Paiz, Joshua. M. 2020b. Preparing Teachers to Create LGBTQ+-inclusive Classrooms. In *Contemporary Foundations for Teaching English as an Additional Language: Pedagogical Approaches and Classroom Applications*, edited by Joan K. Shin and Polina Vinogradova. New York: Routledge.

Paiz, Joshua M. and Gabrielle Reid. 2019. The Writing Classroom as a Performative Space: Possiblities and Challenges for LGBTQ+ Multilingual Learners. Paper presented at the 2019 meeting of the College Conference on Composition and Communication. Pittsburgh, PA, March 2019.

Paiz, Joshua. M. and Junhan Zhu 2018. Queering the Classroom: A Teacher's Decision and a Student's Response. *TESOL Journal* 9, no. 3: 565–568. https://doi.org/10.1002/tesj.371

Paiz, Joshua. M., Anthony Comeau, Junhan Zhu, Jingyi Zhang, and Agnes Santinao, 2018. Queer Bodies, Queer Lives in China English Contact Literature. *Open Linguistics* 4, no. 1: 147–162. https://doi.org/10.1515/opli-2018-0008

Pandavar, Anjuli and Paiz, Joshua. M. 2017. Queer Voices in the Academy: Politics, Ethics, and Education. Moderated debate presented at the Queer and Ally Society, Shanghai, China.

Pavlenko, Anita. 2001. 'In the World of the Tradition, I was Unimagined': Negotiation of Identities in Cross-cultural Autobiographies. *The International Journal of Bilingualism* 5, no. 3: 317–344.

Pavlenko, Anita and Norton, Bonny. 2007. Imagined Communities, Identity, and English Language Learning. In *International Handbook of English Language Teaching*, edited by Jim Cummins and Chris Davison, 669–680. Boston, MA: Springer.

Pawelczyk, Joanna, Łukasz Pakuła and Jane Sunderland. 2014. Issues of Power in Relation to Gender and Sexuality in the EFL Classroom: An Overview. *Journal of Gender and Power* 1, no. 1: 49–66.

Pennycook, Alistair. 2001. *Critical Applied Linguistics: A Critical Introduction*. New York: Routledge.

Pennycook, Alistair. 2006. Critical Applied Linguistics. In *The Handbook of Applied Linguistics*, edited by Alan Davies and Catherine Elder, 784–807. Malden, MA: Wiley-Blackwell.

Pigozzi, Mary. J. 2006. A UNESCO View of Global Citizenship Education. *Educational Review* 58, no. 1: 1–4. https://doi.org/10.1080/00131910500352473

Pinello, Daniel. R. 2006. *America's Struggle for Same-sex Marriage.* Cambridge: Cambridge University Press.

Podos, Rebecca. 2017. *Like Water*. New York: Balzer + Bray.

Pulver, Andrew. 2015. Kansas Teacher won't Resign after Parents Complain over Anti-bullying Film. *The Guardian*, 6 November. Accessed on 7 March 2019. www.theguardian.com/film/2015/nov/06/kansas-schoolteacher-not-resigning-bullying-film

Quinlan, Casey. 2016. This is how Americans Learn LGBT Hate Starting at a Young Age. *Think Progress.* https://thinkprogress.org/this-is-how-americans-learn-lgbt-hate-starting-at-a-young-age-c0afd75e9505/

Rhodes, Christy. M. and James Coda. 2017. It's Not in the Curriculum: Adult English Language Teachers and LGBQ Topics. *Adult Learning* 28, no. 3: 99–106. https://doi.org/10.1177/1045159517712483

Rhodes, Jacqueline. 2015. The Failure of Queer Pedagogy [video essay]. *The Writing Instructor* [*Queer and Now* special issue]. http://parlormultimedia.com/twitest/rhodes-2015-03

Richards, Jack. C. 2001. The Role of Textbooks in a Language Program. *RELC Guidelines* 23, no. 2: 12–16.

Richardson, Justin and Peter Parnell. 2015. *And Tango Makes Three.* New York: Little Simon.

Rivers, Ian. 2001. The Bullying of Sexual Minorities at School: Its Nature and Long-term Correlates. *Educational and Child Psychology* 18, no. 1: 33–46. https://doi.org/10.1093/med:psych/9780199387656.003.0011

Rivers, Ian. 2004. Recollections of Bullying at School and their Long-term Implications for Lesbians, Gay men and Bisexuals. *Crisis: Journal of Crisis Intervention and Suicide Prevention* 25, no. 4: 169–175. https://doi.org/10.1027/0227-5910.25.4.169

Rodriguez, Nelson. M. and William F. Pinar, eds. 2007. *Queering Straight Teachers: Discourse and Identity in Education.* New York: Peter Lang.

Rose, Shirley and Irving Weiser 2002. The WPA as Researcher Archivist. In *The Writing Program Administrator's Resource*, edited by Stuart C. Brown and Theresa J. Enos, 275–302. Mahwah, NJ: Lawrence Erlbaum.

Rowlett, Benedict and Brian W. King. 2018. Language Education, Gender, and Sexuality. In *Encyclopedia of Language and Education Vol. 1: Language Policy and Political Issues in Education*, edited by Teresa L. McCarty and Stephen May, 1–13. New York, Springer. https://doi.org/10.1007/978-3-319-02320-5_7-1

Saunston, Helen. 2016. Authenticating Sexual Diversity in School: Examining Sociolinguistic Constructions of Young People's Sexual Identities. *Journal of Language, Identity, and Education* 15, no. 1: 17–31. https://doi.org/10.1080/15348458.2016.1113812

Saunston, Helen. 2017. Language, Sexuality, and Education. In *Discourse and Education: Encyclopedia of Language and Education*, edited by Stanton Wortham, Deoksoon Kim, and Stephen May, 147–159. New York: Springer. https://doi.org/10.1007/978-3-319-02243-7_14

Saunston, Helen. 2018. Language, Sexuality, and Inclusive Pedagogy in TESOL. Presented at Queering TESOL and World Languages Pedagogy: Troubling Norms and Finding Trouble, colloquium organized by James Coda, conducted at the meeting of the American Association for Applied Linguistics, Chicago, IL.

Scruggs, Thomas. E. Margo A. Mastropieri, and Kimberly A. McDuffie. 2007. Co-teaching in Inclusive Classrooms: A Metasynthesis of Qualitative Research. *Exceptional Children* 73, no. 4: 392–416. https://doi.org/10.1177/001440290707300401

Sedgwick, Eve Kosofsky. 2008. *The Epistomology of the Closet*. Berkeley, CA: University of California Press.

Selvadurai, Shayam. 1994. *Funny Boy: A Novel*. San Diego, CA: Harvest Books.

Shardakova, Marya and Anita Pavlenko. 2004. Identity Options in Russian Textbooks. *Journal of Language, Identity, and Education* 3, no. 1: 25–46. https://doi.org/10.1207/s15327701jlie0301_2

Sharma, Preeti. 2012. Historical Background and Legal Status of Third Gender in Indian Society. *International Journal of Research in Economics & Social Sciences* 2, no. 12: 64–71.

Shin, Joan Kang and Polina Vinogradova, eds. 2020/forthcoming. *Contemporary Foundations for Teaching English as an Additional Language: Pedagogical Approaches and Classroom Applications*. New York: Routledge.

Silva, Tony. 1997. On the Ethical Treatment of ESL Writers. *TESOL Quarterly* 31, no. 2: 359–363.

Skilton-Sylvester, Ellen. 2002. Should I Stay or Should I go?: Investigating Cambodian Women's Participation and Investment in Adult ESL Programs. *Adult Education Quarterly* 53, no. 1: 9–26. https://doi.org/10.1177/074171302237201

Smestad, Bjørn. 2018. LGBT Issues in Norwegian Textbooks. *Nordic Journal of Comparative and International Education* 2, no. 4: 4–20. https://doi.org/10.7577/njcie.2208

Stryker, Susan. 2008. Transgender History, Homonormativity, and Disciplinarity. *Radical History Review* Winter 2008, no. 100: 145–157. https://doi.org/10.1215/01636545-2007-026

Sullivan, Nikki. 2003. *A Critical Introduction to Queer Theory*. New York: New York University Press.

Sunderland, Jane. 2000a. Issues in Language and Gender in Second and Foreign Language Education [review article]. *Language Teaching* 33, no. 4: 203–223. https://doi.org/10.1017/s261444800015688

Sunderland, Jane. 2000b. New Understandings of Gender and Language Classroom Research: Texts, Teacher Talk, Student Talk. *Language Teaching Research* 4, no. 2: 149–173. https://doi.org/10.1177/136216880000400204

Tawake, Sandra. 2006. Cultural Rhetoric in Coming-Out Narratives: Witi Ihimaera's *The Uncle's Story*. *World Englishes* 25, no. 3/4: 373–380.

Teaching Tolerance. n.d. What are Gender Stereotypes. www.tolerance.org/classroom-resources/tolerance-lessons/what-are-gender-stereotypes.

ten Dam, Geert and Monique Volman. 2004. Critical Thinking as a Citizenship Competence: Teaching Strategies. *Learning and Instruction* 14, no. 4: 359–379. https://doi.org/10.1016/j.leaninstruc.2004.01.005

TESOL International Association. 2006. *The Pre K-12 English Language Proficiency Standards.* Alexandria, VA: TESOL Press.

Thumboo, Edwin. 2006. Literary Creativity in World Englishes. In *The Handbook of World Englishes*, edited by Braj. B. Kachru, Yamuna Kachru, and Cecil. L. Nelson, 405–427. Hoboken, NJ: Blackwell Publishing.

Tulsan, Meredith. 2014. 45 Years after Stonewall, the LGBT Movement has a Transphobia Problem. *The American Prospect*, 25 June. Accessed on 6 February 2018. Retrieved from: http://prospect.org/article/45-years-after-stonewall-lgbt-movement-has-transphobia-problem

Ullman, Jacqueline and Tania Ferfolja. 2016. The Elephant in the (Class)room: Parental Perception of LGBTQ-inclusivity in K-12 Educational Contexts. *Australian Journal of Teacher Education* 41, no. 10: 15–29. https://doi.org/10.14221/ajte.2016v41n10.2

UMD Equity Center. n.d. Good Practices: Inclusive Language. University of Maryland LGBT Equity Center. Accessed 6 March 2019. https://lgbt.umd.edu/good-practices-inclusive-language

University of Toledo. 2017. Basic ESL Tutorial. https://engl.utoledo.edu/uttesl/?page_id=9.

Vandrick, Stephanie. 1997. The Role of Hidden Identities in the Postsecondary ESL Classroom. *TESOL Quarterly* 31, no. 1: 153–157. https://doi.org/10.2037/3587980

Vandrick, Stephanie. 2001. Teaching Sexual Identity in the ESL Classroom. Paper presented at the 35th annual meeting of Teaching English to Speakers of Other Languages (TESOL), 28 February, Saint Louis, MO.

Vygotsky, Lev. S. 1978. *Mind in Society: The Development of Higher Psychological Processes*, revised ed. Cambridge, MA: Harvard University Press.

Waggoner, Erin. B. 2018. Bury your Gays and Social Media Fan Response: LGBTQ Representation and Communitarian Ethics. *Journal of Homosexuality* 65, no. 13: 1877–1892. https://doi.org/10.1080/00918369.2017.1391015

Waite, Stacey. 2017. *Teaching Queer: Radical Possibilities for Writing and Knowing.* Pittsburgh, PA: University of Pittsburgh Press.

Watson, Ryan. J., Christopher W. Wheldon, and Stephen T. Russell. 2015. How does Sexual Identity Disclosure Impact School Experiences? *Journal of LGBT Youth* 12, no. 4: 385–396. https://doi.org/10.1080/19361653.2015.1077764

Weinstein, Carol. S. 1981. Classroom Design as an External Condition for Learning. *Educational Technology* 21, no. 8: 12–19.

Weiss, Jillian. T. 2004. GL vs. BT: The Archeology of Biphobia and Transphobia in the US Gay and Lesbian Community. *Journal of Bisexuality* 3, no. 3–4: 25–55.

Welcoming Schools. 2019. Great Diverse Books for your School, Library, or Home. www.welcomingschools.org/resources/books

Winans, Amy. 2006. Queering Pedagogy in the English Classroom: Engaging with the Places where Thinking Stops. *Pedagogy* 6, no. 1: 103–122.

Xu, Zhichang. 2001. Problems and Strategies for Teaching English in Large Classes in the People's Republic of China. *Horizons in Teaching and Learning: Proceedings of the 10th Annual Teaching and Learning Forum*, 7–9. Perth, Australia: Curtin University.

Yang, Lajlim. 2012. *The Construction of a Queer Community in NS-NNS Talk.* Hawaii Pacific University TESOL Working Paper Series 10: 54–64. Honolulu, HI: Hawai'i Pacific University.

Zach, J. Alexandra Mannheim, and Michael Alfano. 2010. 'I Didn't Know What to Say ...': Four Archetypal Responses to Homophobic Rhetoric in the Classroom. *High School Journal* 93, no. 3: 98–110. https://doi.org/10.1353/hsj.0.0047

Index

Note: italic page numbers indicate figures; bold page numbers indicate tables; numbers containing *n* refer to notes.

www.ingramcontent.com/pod-product-compliance
Lightning Source LLC
LaVergne TN
LVHW010444080826
844660LV00026B/1216

9781781797945